Living in the
Corporate Zoo

What is self-evident is that we are in a period of fundamental change. The institutions, social structures and life styles of the old industrial order are breaking down but there are uncertainties as to what are replacing them. New contradictions are emerging such as those of globalisation and the appeal of localism. There are forces of convergence shaping the social structures of different societies while at the same time, pressures that are reinforcing national, regional and local differences.

Is this the kind of society that Britain wants to be in the future? Or should we look to those other countries in Europe that are embracing the challenges of the Information Age but with perspective, social inclusion and quality of life as the endgame?

Living in the Corporate Zoo

Richard Scase

CAPSTONE

Copyright © Richard Scase 2002

The right of Richard Scase to be identified as the author of this work has been asserted in accordance with the Copyright, Designs and Patents Act 1988

First published 2002 by
Capstone Publishing Limited (A Wiley Company)
8 Newtec Place
Magdalen Road
Oxford OX4 1RE
United Kingdom
http://www.capstoneideas.com

CIP catalogue records for this book are available from the British Library and the US Library of Congress

ISBN 1-84112-187-8

Designed and typeset by Baseline, Oxford, UK
Printed and bound by T.J. International
This book is printed on acid-free paper

Substantial discounts on bulk quantities of Capstone books are available to corporations, professional associations and other organisations.

Please contact Capstone for more details on +44 (0)1865 798 623 or (fax) +44 (0)1865 240 941
or (e-mail) info@wiley-capstone.co.uk

Contents

SECTION 5 : A ZOO OF LIFESTYLE TRIBES

SECTION 6 : CYNICAL CITIZENS : THE CHANGING CITIZEN MIX

CONCLUSION

Richard Scase

Richard Scase is Europe's leading business strategist and forecaster and was voted European Business Speaker of the Year in 2002. He is author of the highly influential *Britain in 2010: The New Business Landscape* (Capstone Publishing, 2000), which has not only received wide media attention across the globe but has also contributed to UK government planning and strategy.

Richard regularly addresses senior level executives at company and industry-wide seminars, conferences and management development programmes. He is highly sought after for his views on the changing business environment, creative thinking in management and how future socio-economic and global trends are likely to affect business strategies.

He is also an entrepreneur in his own right having set up a number of successful businesses including a media company, which, after going public, is now part of the Capital Group in the United Kingdom. Most recently, he founded a B2B business, which provides on-line learning materials for corporate management development programmes.

Richard is exclusively represented by:

SPEAKERS for BUSINESS
1-2 Pudding Lane
London EC3R 8AB
United Kingdom
Tel: +44 (0)20 7929 5559
Fax: +44 (0)20 7929 5558
Email: richard.scase@sfb.co.uk
Website: www.britain2010.com

Preface

This is a rather unusual book. It is *not* meant to be read from beginning to end. It consists of a number of short, self-contained pieces, each of which can either be read independently or in sequence. For instance, it can be dipped into at whatever point while waiting for a bus or train. Alternatively, it should be possible to read the whole thing on a flight between Athens or Stockholm and London Heathrow (allowing for a thirty-minute air traffic control delay). The book is the result of a suggestion put to me by Mark Allin of Capstone Wiley. He had seen me give a number of corporate presentations and felt that I should put down some of my ideas on paper. Many of these stem from work I have undertaken for the Economic and Social Research Council, analysing data collected in the British Household Panel Study. But, primarily, this book is written for senior and middle corporate leaders who are having to tackle many of the human challenges associated with large-scale corporate change. Just as technologies are changing the ways we do business, so too are the attitudes and values of people as employees, consumers and citizens. Here, a revolution is occurring that is having just as major an impact on business as the much-hyped Internet.

Many thanks are due to the corporate delegates who, in both private and public sector organisations, have stimulated me with their ideas over the past few years. Thanks are also due to Mark Allin of Capstone, as well as to Nicola Simmons for tidying up my word-processing skills and to Ray Newsam for his technical support, both for my corporate events and for the diagrams in this book.

1

Living in the Global Cage

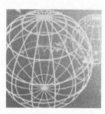

Living in the Global Cage

The revolution in information and communications technologies is restructuring the global economy. These forces of change are affecting the functioning of national economies, the role of governments and the ways in which we work and live. No one is unaffected by these trends, whether they are located in remote villages in sub-Saharan Africa or in the world's great metropolitan centres. The products we use in our everyday lives, the tools and the skills that we employ in our jobs, are all affected by the direct and indirect processes of the technological revolution and globalisation. On a daily basis, we drive automobiles designed in Europe, and manufactured in South-East Asia by companies that are U.S. owned. Our domestic technologies are assembled with components manufactured by subcontractors distributed over all five continents. Their activities are coordinated on a global basis through the application of Internet technologies and corporate decision-making processes.

The products we use in our every day lives, the tools and the skills that we employ in our jobs are all affected by the direct and indirect processes of the technological revolution and globalisation.

Economic cycles are no longer confined to national economies. Regional trade blocs, the operation of currency markets and the world's stock markets have created global interdependencies between countries. Recession in the United States quickly reverberates around the rest of the world. As part of the process of global convergence, the growing dominance of (mainly U.S.-based) multinational corporations plays a key role in shaping our own personal economic circumstances. Corporate 'downsizing' decisions taken in San Francisco, Chicago or New York can instantly generate large-scale unemployment in towns and villages in countries as far ranging as Mexico, Scotland, Sweden and Thailand. These same corporate decisions have further ramifications for the survival of other small businesses through the subsequent downturn in local consumer spending.

The skills we need to succeed and survive in this corporate zoo are equally affected by these global trends. The explosion in information and communication technologies, the revolution in transportation systems and the standardisation of business practices have brought about a shift of the world's manufacturing base to south China and South-East Asia. The skills that we use as employees in Europe and the United States are those needed for the rapidly expanding information and knowledge-based industries. Alternatively, they are the skills required for 'servicing' the personal needs of highly qualified workers as found in the retail, hospitality or (still expanding) state-owned health and welfare sectors. Education systems are compelled to respond to changing skill requirements as driven by globalisation and the information and communications revolution.

Our leisure and recreation activities are equally affected. The tools and equipment that we use are likely to be manufactured in the Far East; the barbecues, the garden furniture and the flowerpots on the house decks or patios will be made in China; the stereo systems, the televisions and other home appliances in South Korea, Malaysia and Taiwan. But the content, the music we listen to, the television shows and the films that we watch will be inspired, if not licensed, mainly by U.S. companies. It is the media that has created the global village. Deregulation and the privatisation of radio and television services throughout the world have created business opportunities that multinational corporations have exploited. This has resulted in global citizens, in particular young people. Each country may continue to have its own entertainment heroes but superimposed upon these, in a globalised hierarchy, are the Hollywood movie stars and the celebrities of the popular music industry. There may be cultural diversity between nations but, as far as the corporate elite is concerned, their lifestyles are homogenised around common conversation pieces that include golf, stock values, the Internet and the capabilities (or not) of third-generation mobile telephone technology.

Today, between one-third and one-half of young people in the United States and Europe attend university. They do so to acquire the skills needed to be the future high earners in the global-based knowledge economy. In their gap years and during vacations, they travel abroad. They are global citizens who regard time zones and national boundaries as airline time distances. Through this means they recognise not only cultural differences between countries but also the forces that are bringing about their convergence. They appreciate how a global cage is incorporating and shaping diverse work and lifestyle practices around the world. For the majority, it is a process to be embraced, while for others it is to be resisted and repelled.

Even so, for all of us, globalisation is shaping the nature of our personal relations. Developments in the world economy over the past fifty years have generated large-scale migration between countries. The result is that, within our families we have kin – as sons, daughters, brothers, sisters, grandchildren, stepchildren – whose personal heritage is steeped in other cultures. A paradox of the global cage is that it has broken down national and regional parochialisms. But through its centrifugal impact, it has generated greater diversity within our own personal lifestyles. We may be global citizens using similar technologies at work. In our everyday lives we may admire the same celebrities, but we are not all the same. Globalisation has created, strangely enough, greater individuality and cultural diversity. We exercise greater choices in our spending patterns, personal relations and our lifestyles. The paradox is that as we become more similar, we also become more different from each other.

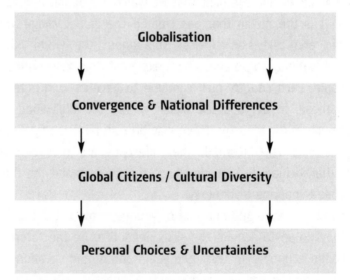

Essentially, convergence, globalisation and the emergence of the global village are a process of Americanisation. Products may be manufactured in South-East Asia and there may be indigenous industrial sectors in Europe, but it is the United States, as the world's largest economy and the national base for the greater majority of the world's largest corporations that is the global driver. These companies created more wealth in the latter half of the twentieth century than the whole of humankind preceding 1950. This will continue in the future – except at a faster pace – and, as the Manhattan atrocity has shown, creating growing resentment among those excluded from these wealth-generating processes.

The interconnective world and competitive clusters

Our lives may be shaped by global forces, which may be standardising many aspects of our work and lifestyles, but these same forces are creating national, regional and local differences in personal opportunities and life chances. An interconnected world is creating an international division of labour. This is generating differences between countries as separate nations compete with each other to attract foreign direct investment for economic growth and renewal.

Global forces are creating national, regional and local differences in personal opportunities and life chances.

Low-technology industries are locating in South-East Asia and, in the future, increasingly, south China. The advantages are clear: low labour costs, a favourable governmental environment and the absence of oppositional trade unionism. But these are integrated within global supply chains that now operate with just-in-time efficiency as a result of the information and communications-technology revolution. It is easily forgotten that the key drivers for the development of Internet technologies are multinational corporations with their need to manage effectively their worldwide supply chains. It will continue to be B2B transactions that will generate Internet revenue growth rather than the dubious business case of B2C.

Economic activities have always been clustered in particular geographical locations. In the past, this was driven by the local availability of raw materials, energy sources and transport facilities. This was the case with the industrial revolutions in the United States and Europe, which shaped the economic development of, for example, Pittsburgh, Chicago, Glasgow, Alsace Lorraine and the Ruhr Valley.

The difference today with the location of economic activities in different regions of the world is that these processes are driven by global, rather than by local, forces. Corporate senior

Globalisation

80% of global economic activity is generated in the 20 richest countries
◆ In the industrialised world (OECD)
  – *350 million are employed*
But...
◆ In the developing world
  – *There will be an extra 700 million workers wanting jobs in the next 20 years*

managers treading the global stage dictate investment decisions that shape local economic growth, rather than the profitable market opportunities identified by local born and bred entrepreneurs. The global corporate capitalists of today have none of their entrepreneurial predecessors' affinity or social responsibility to local communities. Profit-making centres are set up and demolished according to short-term (Q1, Q2 and Q3) calculations that create cultures of anxiety among employees. This happens even in the most self-confident corporations trading in what appear to be ever-growing market segments. The cutbacks in head count in technology, media and telecommunications companies in 2000 and 2001 are a token of the vulnerability we all now experience in our jobs.

With economic clustering, national economies are becoming more specialised, with their focus upon particular activities. In the United States and Europe, the focus is on high-technology and information services, but the drivers of growth in these national economies are even more geographically concentrated than their national boundaries would suggest. It is the regional clusters within countries that are becoming more pronounced. California, and clusters around Boston, are centres of gravity for the information and communication industries. So, too, are Antwerp-Brussels in Belgium, Stockholm in Sweden and the Thames Valley in the United Kingdom. The software industry is the prime example of a truly mobile and global activity. But the need to 'localise' products and services for different national business requirements has generated clusters of skills around Dublin in the Republic of Ireland.

Changing global context

Growth of regional and national specialisation in global supply chains

- Singapore   – Value-added logistics
- Italy   – Design
- India   – Software
- Asia   – Manufacture
- United States   – Information Services
- Africa   – Commodities and Agriculture
- South America   – Commodities and Manufacture
- Europe   – High Technology
- Middle East   – Oil and Intellectual Capital

The interconnected world has abolished the traditional distinction between developed and developing countries. India is the prime example of this. The software industry in India is expected to grow to $90 bn of exports by 2008. By then, there will be more Indian technology graduates than the total population of the United Kingdom. This industry is predominantly located in Bangalore and Hyderabad, and functions alongside traditional forms of agricultural and village lifestyles that have been relatively unchanged for centuries.

Around Accra in Ghana, a similar pattern is emerging as companies in Europe and the United States download their back-office data-processing activities. In Central America, the value of Costa Rica's software exports is greater than that generated by its sale of coffee. In the Siberian region of Russia, the town of Novosibirsk is emerging as a centre for software design through outsourcing by German corporations.

In this interconnected world, towns and regions compete with each other to win the business on offer from the world's major corporations. These location decisions and, therefore, directly or indirectly our own jobs, are shaped by a number of considerations. English-language ability is one key variable. This is one of the major reasons for the attractions of India. But the availability of cheap brainpower, produced by national education systems is also a determining factor. National economies compete with each other in this, together with the usual tax breaks and other set-up subsidies. Corporations, as the purchasers of educated labour, can pick and choose locations on a global basis. However, unlike the local entrepreneurs of the past, their commitment to any particular place is, at best, only temporary and short term. The employees of Motorola in Scotland and Ericsson in the different countries of Europe have experienced this in the recent past.

The regional specialisation of economic clusters is creating divisions within national economies. This is as much the case in the United States as in Europe, China, Russia and the countries of the Far East and Central America. Economic inequalities are emerging between occupations that are generating regional imbalances. These are affecting the provision of social, recreational and welfare amenities that, in turn, are the drivers of national and international population migration patterns. California continues to grow, as do the south-east of the United Kingdom and the Malmo-Copenhagen region of Scandinavia. Other areas within these national hinterlands decline, creating poverty, economic dependency and social exclusion. How far can national governments resist these pressures if their high-tax, social-inclusion policies are unacceptable to the treasurers of large corporations? The competitive advantage of nations in an interconnected wired world relegates the role of national governments to passive providers of infrastructures. In a global economy there appears to be no 'third way'.

A wired world and interconnected protest

Convergence between economies has been driven by the growth of multinational corporations, globally-based media industries and worldwide supply chains. New business models are emerging that make traditional distinctions and divisions irrelevant. 'Small' and 'large' companies are no longer separate categories of economic activity. Both types of business are integrated within global trading activities. Small firms are capable of operating as international businesses while multinationals, operating as global brands, function as groupings of devolved, decentralised entrepreneurial units.

New business models are emerging that make traditional distinctions and divisions irrelevant. 'Small' and 'large' companies are no longer separate categories of economic activity.

Within this global economy, corporations are highly mobile. Companies can transfer their trading activities between national economies depending upon incentive environments as enabled by national governments. It becomes the responsibility of state regimes to create national competitive advantage through providing attractive infrastructures, human resources and fiscal environments. The outcome is the repositioning of national governments as facilitators of economic growth and employment opportunities rather than, as in the twentieth century, the key providers of these. Privatisation and deregulation of industrial sectors are the direct outcome of this readjustment, generated by the forces of globalisation.

For individuals, the consequences are greater feelings of vulnerability, anxiety and being 'out of control'. This is in sharp contrast to the old economic order. The earlier part of the twentieth century witnessed the growth of large corporations, but these were mainly manufacturing companies located according to the availability of national resources, labour and transport facilities. Because of these factors, their location was fixed and their potential to relocate highly limited. The under-development of information and communication technologies and global transport systems reinforced this. This concentration of economic production led to the growth of the trade-union movement, working-class consciousness and social democratic political parties. In Russia, it brought about the Communist revolution and the later imposition of state socialism in the countries of central Europe. In the rest of Europe, working-class solidarity led to calls for either the state ownership of the means of production or the regulation of capitalist enterprises through high levels of government intervention.

In the global economy of today, the mobility of capital and the shifting of manufacturing facilities to South-East Asia has destroyed the basis for working-class solidarity. The decline of large-scale manufacturing facilities in the United States and Europe has eroded the potential for trade unionism and other forms of collective support. The outcome for these information-based economies is the spread of cultures of individualism. No longer can we rely upon the support of others. In the corporate zoo of the twenty-first century, we have to take care of ourselves.

Employees of today need transferable skills that enable them to shift from one employer to the next. Continuous life-long learning becomes a personal priority as we are compelled to change jobs as we migrate from Pennsylvania to California, from Hamburg to Bonn, from Liverpool to London. As employees, we are constantly aware of the vulnerability of our life chances to corporation decision-making. A recent event in northern Sweden illustrates this very common experience. In a small village, a local mechanic developed an innovative wood cutting machine. He set up a factory in the village that grew to employ sixty people, the majority of the local labour force. Five years ago, Caterpillar purchased the business with the promise of creating more jobs. Within two years, it had closed the whole operation and shifted its manufacturing facilities elsewhere.

Globalisation has created opportunities for personal mobility and personal advancement. Migration both between and within countries is the result of people searching for better jobs. Migration into the European Union has averaged one million per year over the past ten years. The influx of migrants from Mexico is of a magnitude that is changing the business and political cultures of California. The growth of the Spanish-speaking population is creating business opportunities for entrepreneurial ventures just as it is changing the nature of personnel practices in large corporations.

But there is a paradox. Forces of convergence within the world economic order are generating new forms of protest. In an interconnected wired world, the protests of individuals can take on a global dimension. The 'love bug' generated by a teenager in the Philippines in 1999 corrupted the software of major corporations around the world. How long will it be before software engineers in India act to paralyse the banking systems of the United States and the United Kingdom in support of their demands for higher wages? The paradox in a wired world is that just as individuals are more vulnerable to the actions of large corporations so, too, are the latter more susceptible to the actions of individuals. The protest of a few has the potential to bring large corporations to their knees. The militancy of the trade unions of the past was insignificant in its consequences compared with the capabilities now available to those operating with key computer-based skills in the Information Age. It is irrelevant compared with what international terrorists can do when they target a major financial centre like Manhattan.

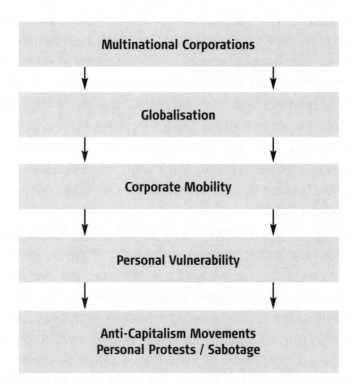

The impact of corporate brands is significant in this. Coca-Cola, McDonalds, General Motors and Ford are, for many, symbols of globalisation or more precisely, of the dominance of the United States. They are seen to represent the ways in which modern corporations are destroying the environment, exploiting the world's population and inhibiting global sustainability.

The information economies of the United States and Europe, with their highly educated human resources, are societies where consumers demand increasing information about the nature of the products that they buy. They insist upon transparency and traceability in terms of product origins, composition and the conditions under which they are manufactured. This ranges from foodstuffs and footwear, to drugs and electronic products. In an interconnected world, the vulnerability of companies to these consumer anxieties is enhanced. The speed at which protest can be transmitted around the world through Internet and other communication technologies is unprecedented. Monsanto has been unable to recover from its experiments with genetic agriculture in Europe. Nike continues to get bad PR for its use of labour in South-East Asia, while Pfizer's reputation has been battered by its approach to the sale of drugs in Africa.

In this wired world, meetings of corporate leaders and heads of states in Seattle, London, Gothenburg and Genoa become focal points for direct political action. Just as with the major corporate brands, these meetings symbolically represent the dominant forces of convergence and globalisation. The new economic order of the twenty-first century necessitates these meetings. They also illustrate the need for effective international regulatory bodies that are more than puppets of United States governments, whose funding is ultimately dependent upon lobbying by forceful economic pressure groups. Otherwise, direct protest will increase as younger world citizens regard the new economic order as 'out of order'.

Globalisation and the reinvented business

The interconnected world is changing the nature of business transactions. This change is both in terms of internal business operations and in their relations with others in ever-changing markets. Customer relations and business partnerships between manufacturers, suppliers and retailers are being re-engineered through the capabilities of Internet technologies.

Customer relations and business partnerships between manufacturers, suppliers and retailers are being re-engineered through the capabilities of Internet technologies.

These technologies allow suppliers, manufacturers and retailers to collaborate in the development of innovative products and services. They allow for cost-effective inventory management among retailers, as well as for lean production systems for manufacturers. These factors, combined with flexible assembly processes, make it possible for global corporations to produce personalised goods. In the purchase of automobiles, the consumer places an order with a detailed specification of his or her requirements. The car retailer then feeds this to the manufacturer which, in turn, schedules production on the basis of placing component orders with their globally distributed suppliers.

In food retailing, it means the end of seasons and seasonal purchasing patterns. No longer are personal dietary intakes shaped by the sale of particular vegetables at certain times of the year. In Europe, there is now all-year-round availability of new potatoes, fresh strawberries and tomatoes. At the same time, what were once regarded as exotic food products are now taken-for-granted supermarket stock items. We complain and shift our custom to rival retailers if there are no mangoes, lemons, avocados and pomegranates on the shelves in January. However, it has become even more detailed and sophisticated than this. Large retailers now hire weather forecasters to given them projections of daily, weekly and monthly temperature and sunshine patterns. On the basis of these projections, orders are placed for different foodstuffs with producers located around the world. Fruit and vegetables can be picked, transported and placed on superstore shelves on the other side of the globe within 24 to 36 hours. *farmers*

Seasonal differences in sporting enjoyment are similarly disappearing. The entertainment industry is now structured as global supply chains, with national broadcasters purchasing their programming content from a broad range of specialist service providers. Tennis, athletics and golf have become global, year-round viewing sports. So, too, has cricket for the English-speaking world (with the exception of the United States). Similar trends are occurring for motor racing and soccer (again with the exception of the United States). The challenge for broadcasters is now to negotiate with event organisers and commercial sponsors the scheduling of programming so that peak audiences are reached across different time zones. It means that Manchester United play Liverpool in the football premiership at 12 noon (instead of 3 pm) in order to reach peak-time viewers in the southern hemisphere. *Making things popular*

The leisure styles of populations in the United States and Europe have been greatly transformed by global supply chains that incorporate small-scale manufacturers in China with multiple retailers. In the past, outdoor garden furniture was expensive and sold as a luxury product. Today, a mass market has emerged in garden tables and chairs, barbecues, grills, etc, and other DIY goods.

In whatever sphere of commerce – manufacturing, food and household-goods retailing, sport or entertainment – the key forces shaping the emergence of global supply chains have been cross-border corporate mergers and acquisitions. These have created today's global businesses that are able to dictate the dynamics of global supply chains. It is their need to coordinate their trading relations with business partners that has been a key force in shaping the development of Internet technologies. Without a sustainable business case, the Internet would have remained the preserve of the United States military establishment and the world's academic institutions.

These same technologies are creating greater opportunities for small entrepreneurial ventures. The Internet allows for small firms to participate in global supply chains, delivering products and services to larger corporations. It allows them to operate, in their own right, as international businesses. Software-design companies in remote locations in the South Pacific can function as service providers to large corporations in the northern hemisphere. MBA graduates, trained at U.S. universities, return to the more remote parts of China with business ideas. With

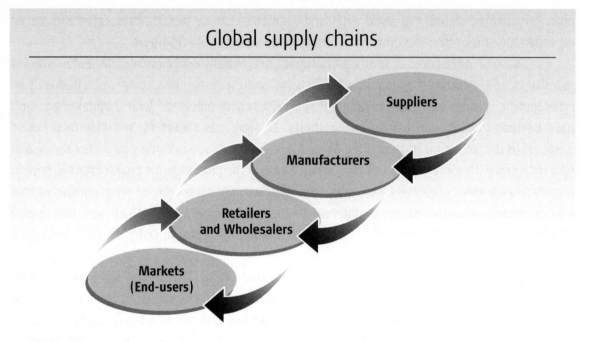

Global supply chains

these, they research market opportunities in the different regions of the world, negotiate with import/export agencies and proceed to set up small-scale manufacturing facilities. They become part of the global economic order.

At the same time, the potential for corporate exploitation becomes more acute. Enterprise zones created in South-East Asia can function as 'fronts' for the use of under-age labour and for the payment of excessively low wages to women and other vulnerable groups protected by neither ective state regimes nor trade unionism. Major companies can maintain a one-step distance from such conditions through the use of local subcontractors and other service providers. It is fast becoming the responsibility of consumers, investigative journalists and international agencies to uncover exploitative employment conditions. Once exposed, this knowledge is rapidly transmitted on a global basis, often doing irreparable damage to what were once regarded as respectable, socially responsible corporate brands.

Such developments are fundamentally changing the ways we do business. The creation of global supply chains, together with the emergence of specialised regional economic clusters, is bringing about the fundamental restructuring of the internal operating processes of large corporations. Increasingly, they are breaking themselves up as integrated operating structures. The trend is for manufacturers to reinvent themselves as brand-management corporations. Their strategy is to outsource and to focus upon only a key set of core competencies. But what is the brand to represent and how is this to be marketed? The shift is away from corporate brands that are allied to particular products and services. Instead, the emphasis is upon corporate branding that conveys experiences, images and sensory experiences. Products are marketed on the basis of their intangible, rather than their tangible, attributes. Benetton promotes its clothing on the basis of marketing campaigns that emphasise outrageousness (poster campaigns) and excitement (motor racing). Coca-Cola promotes itself using an appeal to authenticity ('the real thing'). Camel

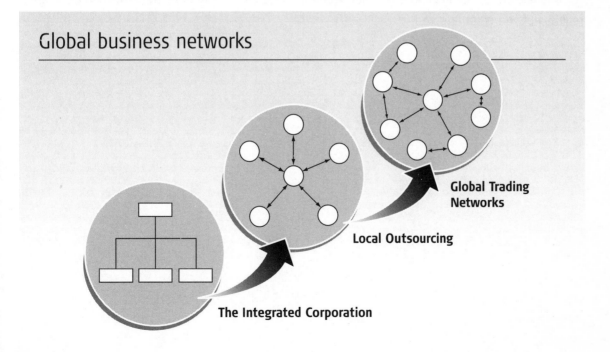

Global business networks

Global Trading
Networks

Local Outsourcing

The Integrated Corporation

cigarettes on the appeal to live life to the full (outdoor sports, taking risks, 'it's your life' and so smoke if you want to).

By constructing corporate brands that convey experiences (quality of life, authenticity, trust, etc) instead of focusing upon the tangible qualities of their specific products and services, companies are able to keep their options open for the future. It allows them continually to reinvent their product portfolios. This they are able to do because of their management of supply chains. Suppliers and manufacturers of one particular good or service can be replaced by others. As consumer preferences change, so too large corporations can continually reinvent their product portfolios in response. Operating under a consistent brand umbrella, new products and services can be delivered. The consequence is that the modern corporation has constantly to be alert to changes in customer and consumer preferences and needs. The fact that they are able to respond so rapidly to these is due to their flexible management of supply chains through Internet technologies and customer-focused management cultures. It reinforces the constantly changing realities of the corporate zoo.

Advertising the product

The reinvented business: in-house or out?

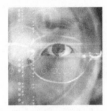

The Internet gives companies the ability to coordinate diverse activities through shared information systems and data processing. It allows companies to reduce their cost structures and enables them to concentrate upon their core skills as manufacturers, suppliers and retailers. The Internet makes for collaborative relations between companies so that information can be shared for product development, inventory management and lean delivery systems.

The Internet makes for collaborative relations between companies so that information can be shared for product development, inventory management and lean delivery systems.

The outcome is the emergence of business networks consisting of companies in strategic alliances and joint ventures with each other with the outsourcing of non-strategic, core activities to business partners and various franchising and licensing arrangements. It is the *What we Are* restructuring of business transactions, on the basis of long-term strategic partnerships, that creates opportunities for many entrepreneurial ventures. The outsourcing of corporate activities has allowed specialist service providers to establish themselves. It is for this reason that entrepreneurial clusters have emerged within different global and national regions. The best-known example, of course, is California, where investment by large corporations in productive capacity has generated opportunities for business start-up through joint ventures and collaborative investment. Around Dublin, investment by global high-technology companies has created an entrepreneurial culture in which start-ups have flourished, focused upon 'localising' software products for different European markets.

Even so, in these reinvented businesses, what is to be outsourced and what to be retained in-house? Each business develops its own strategies according to its own product and market portfolios. The outcome is that there are some pharmaceutical companies that no longer manufacture compounds but concentrate on research, development and clinical trials. There are

What the Human needs to Survive in this Modernizing world of Technical Sciences

Strategic alliances and partnerships

Strategic customer relationships

Partnerships for broad and related product portfolios

Partnerships for product Innovation

others that have pursued quite the reverse strategy. What is a determining factor is the positioning of companies within their own business networks. Through partnering and sharing each other's capabilities, each company is able to identify and emphasise its own particular competencies.

One of these competencies is the development of core skills on the basis of customer knowledge. This is one function that cannot be outsourced. The collection and analysis of customer data, whether these are manufacturers, retailers or end-user consumers, is the basis for product innovation and development. This data, once translated into corporate intelligence, allows companies to be agile in the constant renewal of their product portfolios. 3-M is a classic example of such a business, as are BP, Vivendi Universal and Centrica. Centrica was once a UK state-owned utility company (British Gas). Today, on the basis of its customer knowledge, it has become a highly diversified service provider, ranging from automobile breakdown retrieval and home insurance, to credit cards and domestic repairs.

However, the risks are high. An exclusive preoccupation with customer data management can lead to an over-excessive focus upon present-day consumer wishes leading to the neglect of customer future needs. Information about consumer behaviour today may offer little information about developing marketing and sales strategies for the future. Companies can be *too close* to their customers. This can prevent them from anticipating future consumer needs driven by changing demographics, lifestyles and purchasing preferences. This is a problem facing the UK retailer, Marks and Spencer. Its portfolio of clothing products has failed to keep pace with the changing purchasing preferences of its 'middle-aged' core customers as driven by their shift from 'comfortable' to 'fashion' clothes. This alerts us to the dangers of over-complacent assumptions about the value and strength of corporate brands. There is the constant need to extol the values of the brand and to deliver products and services accordingly. It is a function that cannot be outsourced to public relations companies and advertising experiences. But corporate branding is also important for managing relations with shareholders and employees. The growth of private investors and the rapid expansion of mutual funds in the United States and in Europe, compels companies to present themselves to shareholders as socially responsible and committed to the environment and economic sustainability. Failure to promote the corporate brand according to such criteria can affect stock values, capitalisation and opportunities for future corporate funding. The remuneration of directors, if regarded as excessive, can brand businesses as greedy, selfish and socially irresponsible.

Corporate branding is equally important for good employee relations. It is fast becoming a fact of life that the majority of employees in the Information Age will be university graduates. They are attracted to companies that are committed to socially responsible values, offer opportunities for personal growth and encourage personal creativity, innovation and experimentation. Software companies, over the past few years, have been able to portray these values enabling them to select the most talented graduates.

In reinvented businesses, most functions are undertaken in partnership with others within strategic networks, but what is the glue that holds each individual company together? The need arises to nurture the corporate heart and soul. Employees need emotional engagement, a psychological attachment that extends beyond financial rewards and other material incentives. This demands that corporate leaders nurture corporate affiliation through culture building and sociability.

A paradox of the wired world and the e-corporation is that the nurturing of human relations and the psychological contract with employees becomes more, rather than less, important.

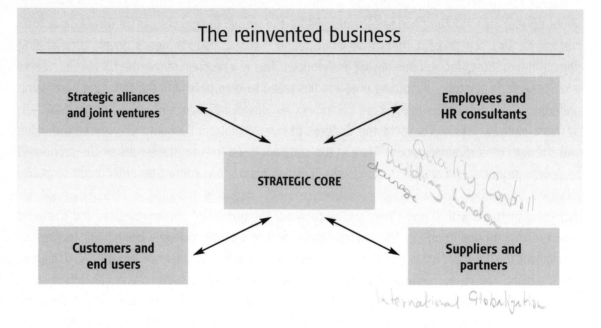

This point is well illustrated by the experience of GlaxoSmithKline. The morale of the catering staff is vital to the success of the company's drug discovery process. If their morale is high, good quality food is served in the staff restaurant. This results in scientists using this facility rather than taking snacks to work that they consume privately in their own separate work areas. By eating together in the restaurant, they share ideas and brainstorm. These ideas often become the basis for later detailed analysis and experimentation. Does this example imply that even the catering facilities of a company should not be outsourced? It depends how the partnership is managed. This can either be a pragmatic cost-saving device or a longer-term strategic relationship with a service provider who understands the true nature of the business. Most outsourcing arrangements express the philosophy of the former instead of the latter.

The interconnected corporation:
The reinvented corporate giants

How can the corporate giants respond to the challenges of the wired world? Market barriers are breaking down with deregulation and the lowering of tariffs within different regionally based trading blocs. Competitive pressures are more apparent as accountancy practices and business standards are harmonised on a global basis. ISO 9000, and similar benchmarks, encourage companies to develop global cultures in their internal and external trading practices. Markets are also changing as both customers and consumers are able to exercise greater purchasing choices from a far broader range of service providers. Geographical parameters are widened through Internet trading relations. These are reinforced by the harmonisation of intergovernmental fiscal regimes and the revolution in bulk transportation systems. The sophistication of logistics management techniques, together with the application of bulk containerisation for overland, sea and air transportation has changed the global context for doing business.

Markets are changing as both customers and consumers are able to exercise greater purchasing choices from a far broader range of service providers.

Significant Movement

In this interconnected world, corporate giants are not only in competition with each other but they are often competing with local-based, entrepreneurial ventures. The great corporations of the world may dominate global supply chains but this does not prevent them from being threatened by more adaptive, local operators. How are these global giants to respond to this changing business environment? Their strategies of the past are no longer appropriate for the present or the future. Essentially, historically they used either the *global* or the *multinational* approach. Each is now superceded by the need to have *transnational* operating structures.

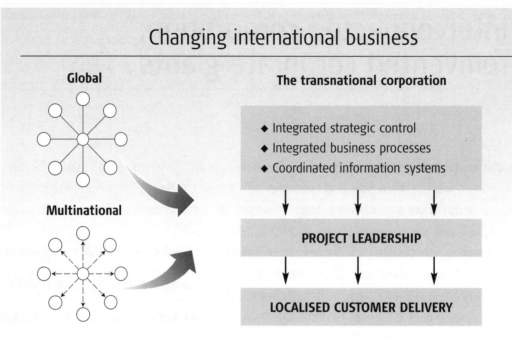

Changing international business

Global

Multinational

The transnational corporation

◆ Integrated strategic control
◆ Integrated business processes
◆ Coordinated information systems

PROJECT LEADERSHIP

LOCALISED CUSTOMER DELIVERY

After: C. Bartlett & S. Ghosal *Managing Across Borders* (1992)

The *global* corporation was highly centralised in both its strategic and operational processes. The great U.S. corporations adhered to this model. Having saturated the home market, they embarked upon developing foreign markets through operating from their national base. IBM is a good case in point. It became a global corporation through developing a standardised product which it then exported to the rest of the world. The strategic assumption was that the requirement for computer mainframes would be the same all over the world. Cultural diversity in business structures and practices was not recognised. If they were, the assumption was that these would evaporate through global convergence, by adopting the U.S. 'way of doing things'.

The result was a corporation where R & D, production, marketing and selling strategies are all concentrated at corporate headquarters. The outcome was a highly centralised, hierarchical corporate structure that served the company well during the 'growth decade' of the 1980s when the demand for corporate mainframes was insatiable. There were enough 'standardised' corporate structures in the world to absorb IBM's products. By the late 1980s, there was a greater recognition of diversity in global business practices and, as a result, the development of a more devolved and flexible operating structure. The pressures were for a shift towards greater corporate decentralisation. That is, the extension of operating autonomy to market-focused business units and for the corporate centre to be more hands-off. So, too, it is with many other companies. The highly centralised global model is no longer appropriate. Companies such as IBM have had to devolve and decentralise but, at the same time, to maintain centralised strategic control.

The *multinational* corporation is structured according to entirely the opposite principles. It is highly decentralised with the corporate centre operating as little more than a treasury and with two major purposes. The first, to approve the business plans of each of the separate operating units that make up the conglomerate. The second is to make acquisitions and divestments. Otherwise, the majority of strategic and operational responsibilities are devolved to each of the separate operating units. This was very much the business model of General Motors, Unilever and Hewlett Packard until the early 1990s. Each business unit operated in a separate national or regional market with its own brand. For General Motors, it was Vauxhall in the UK and Opel in Germany. This is still the case. But, in the past, there would be separate and distinct R & D, manufacturing, marketing and selling functions attached to each of these business units. The outcome of these highly decentralised structures was a high level of customer focus and a very market-responsive R & D activity. However, the downside was high duplication of overheads as the units more or less replicated each other. Market responsiveness was bought at a high price.

Both the *global* and *multinational* business models are now superceded by the transnational corporation. This has been enabled by the growth of intranet and Internet technologies. In fact, the need to shift to transnationalism is a reason for the development of Internet technologies. It is driven by the need for global corporate coordination to deliver products as required by the specific and particular demands of local markets. In the global corporation, decision-making flows are from the centre to each of the operating units. In the multinational business, decision-making is located within each of the operating units. In either model, there is little need for the exchange of information across business units. In the transnational corporation, by contrast, cross-unit and integrated strategic decision-making processes are at the very core of the operation. Transnational companies operate through coordinating the strategic and operational activities that have devolved to each of the separate business units. These companies are both highly centralised and decentralised. Internet technologies allow for the transnational corporation to function as both a global and multinational corporation at the same time. Through the coordination of decentralised strategic and operational activities, corporate resources on a worldwide basis can be leveraged to deliver goods and services as required by the peculiarities of local markets.

The automobile companies, as transnational corporations, coordinate their global resources in this way. Their R & D, manufacturing and procurement functions are harnessed to deliver particular branded products for specific regional and national markets. 'Core global model ranges' are adapted to meet local customer needs. The pharmaceutical companies coordinate their R & D

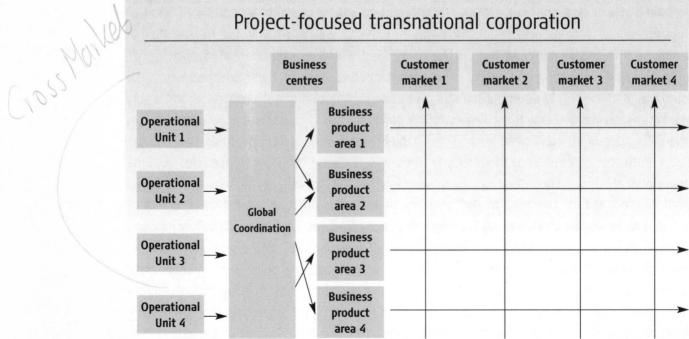

and manufacturing capabilities to deliver healthcare products according to the demands of separate national regulatory authorities. These often stipulate different criteria for clinical trials, product specification, packaging and after-prescription monitoring.

Transnational corporations are global giants but they function as local entrepreneurial fleas. This is creating new business challenges. How do they schedule and prioritise activities between their separate operating units? How do they create global management teams? In the global corporation, the operating culture is imposed from the headquarters of the home country. In the multinational, each unit operates autonomously with its own cultural practices. But, in the transnational corporation, operating processes are structured around global coordination. In this situation, managing cultural diversity across operating units takes precedence. It is this that shapes the design of effective business practices and with it, the use of Internet technologies. The challenges for the transnational corporation are those associated with cultural coordination and harmonisation of operating practices. Without success in these spheres, no effective information system can be implemented and corporate giants fail in their attempts to be customer-focused entrepreneurial fleas in highly diverse, ever changing local markets.

A wired world but the need for face-to-face

[handwritten: Uses reason for Relations with America for hope of survival]

The Internet is changing the ways we work and how we do business. Businesses are competing in a more integrated global marketplace. Large companies are the key drivers in this trend as they reduce their costs through purchasing products, components and different services from suppliers from all regions of the world. The large global players are able to play off service suppliers against each other in their attempts to cut costs and to increase shareholder value. Smaller manufacturing businesses, on the other hand, are subject to greater global competitive pressures, threatening their very survival. What hope do these small businesses in Europe have of competing against lower-cost providers in south China and South-East Asia?

The large global players are able to play off service suppliers against each other in their attempts to cut costs and to increase shareholder value.

In principle, very little but, in practice, a great deal. Although the Internet does offer the technological capabilities for global-based business transactions, the realities of how business is conducted suggest there are severe limits. We should never underestimate the importance of face-to-face, eye-to-eye contact in the execution of business deals. That is why we so often like to do business with local partners rather than with those in other parts of the world. It is also the reason why airport executive lounges remain packed despite the growth of e-business. Even the big global players prefer to conduct their affairs with those whom they deal with face-to-face.

[handwritten: Communication]

At the end of the day, doing business is all about trust relations. This is not only in terms of getting paid for the goods and services provided but, also, in the reliability and quality of delivery processes. It is very easy to get a quote over the Internet for the manufacture of sprockets from a manufacturer in south China, but what happens next? Do we place an order or do we arrange a visit to find out about the company's track record, credibility and quality controls? Will we really put our businesses at risk through relying upon the delivery of parts from an overseas, unknown supplier that we require to deliver completed products to our long-term customers? The Internet revolutionises our ability to source from lower-cost providers and to maintain close operational links with these, as well as allowing us to outsource to businesses in other parts of the world previously unheard of. But it will not lead to the substitution of the human factor. More likely than not, the Internet will generate the need for even greater travel and the necessity to maintain a wider network of personal contacts across a broader spread of the globe.

Throw into the equation differences in the world time zones, and the outcome is even longer working hours and greater work-related stresses for managers and the owners of small firms. Not altogether the rosy picture of the Internet world that the proponents of the Information Age would like us to believe. It is because of the importance of the human factor that the Internet will not render the geographical factor obsolete. In theory, virtual organisations can operate from anywhere in the world so long as there is bandwidth capability and suitable information and communication infrastructures. But companies are finding that their core workers, upon whom they rely for the delivery of innovative, competitive products, attach mounting importance to where they live. They expect quality of life, good local amenities and 'buzz'. In other words, paradoxically, in an increasingly global economy, locality becomes more, rather than less, important. It puts an added responsibility upon local authorities to offer appropriate infrastructures if their communities are not only to thrive but even to survive in an Internet era.

If there are limits to B2B transactions, there are similar human factors that operate against the much predicted take-off of B2C businesses. The dot.com boom has become the dot.com slump, brought about by misplaced assumptions regarding consumer purchasing patterns and the disregard of traditional bricks-and-mortar business principles. In the old economy, we had to be sharp to set up a successful business. It required us to have detailed knowledge and understanding of financial management, marketing skills and selling techniques. These could usually be obtained only through years of hard work and experience in order to identify new business opportunities, as these were driven by changing customer needs. It was necessary to be streetwise, intuitive and to have an in-depth understanding of consumer psychology.

However, for those wanting to set up their own businesses, this was only the beginning of the story. It was also necessary to develop detailed business plans, consisting of sales forecasts, cash-flow projections and estimates of fixed and operating costs. Then came the difficult bit: the need to convince financial backers that we had viable business plans. This meant interview after interview with bank managers for overdraft facilities and knocking on the doors of venture capitalists. Their responses were normally at worst hostile, at best suspicious. But if we were sufficiently good as negotiators, we could just be lucky in persuading them to invest in our business propositions in return for a claim on our houses and a stake in the ownership of our businesses. But only on the condition that we paid high lending and other related management charges. Once these barriers were overcome, we could then start trading and, after several years, we might just begin to think that it had all been worthwhile. If we failed, we lost everything, including our houses and, if we succeeded, the venture capitalists, who risked nothing, would benefit from our years of risk, stress and hard work.

Then came along the new economy, the dot.com business era. Suddenly all the old principles of business start-up were thrown out of the window. Hard-earned experiences and expertise were no longer required. Take the case of Boo.com. All that was needed was a Swedish pretty face and a poetry critic. No need for detailed business plans, financial-control mechanisms and in-depth market assessment of the demand for the products. All that the business required was a few flash presentations to City institutions to raise the funds, a £70 million spend on advertising and promotion and, wow, the pretty face and poetry critic would be the millionaire owners of an on-line global fashion business. Not surprisingly, it has all ended in tears.

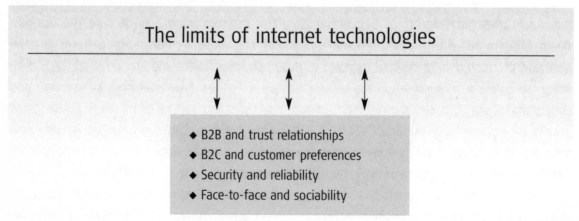

The limits of internet technologies

- ◆ B2B and trust relationships
- ◆ B2C and customer preferences
- ◆ Security and reliability
- ◆ Face-to-face and sociability

There is first the arrogance of it all. The poetry critic and the pretty face presumably assumed that it was entirely unnecessary to gain any retailing skills before embarking upon this venture. Their product was 'urban sportswear'. What is that supposed to be? Is it a trendy word for wearing trainers while shopping in city centres, or have we missed something? Add to this the total ignorance of basic business principles such as, for example, setting up a call centre in an expensive location such as the heart of London. Of course, our trendy Swedes did not feel it necessary to think through the logistic issues associated with the storage and distribution of their products to customers. Instead, they seem to have assumed that the business would roll in by arranging a series of trendy parties around the world for the beautiful 'in-people' who would not have contributed one dollar to generating sales revenue. Add to this the gullibility of the City institutions acting as advisers and sources of funding. What on earth encouraged them to charge into such a venture when the product was so ill-defined and the demand had not been market tested?

And this still continues with the misplaced hype surrounding 3G mobile telephone technologies. Is there really a business case for accessing bank accounts through mobile phones? On-line and wireless retailing is nothing more than a modern version of traditional mail order. This never had much appeal in Europe because of short geographical distances and the ability of people to shop in nearby locations. The reluctance to use mail order was associated with the problem of returning goods and of being at home when they are delivered. Exactly the same problems apply to B2C retailers. But perhaps the major downside of the dot.com boom was that it generated distorted valuations of solid, old-economy stocks and shares.

Businesses with solid trading track records became under-weighted on the world's stock markets and vulnerable to takeover. The ultimate victims of these corporate under-valuations were ordinary citizens in company and occupational pension schemes and those with equity savings. In an era when image and PR take centre-stage, this is of little importance, so long as the dot.com beautiful people are able to seduce gullible financial institutions. But the downside was that, until the retail trading potential of the Internet was put into proper perspective, the world's major financial markets were highly distorted. We still live with the legacy today, with economic downturn, even before 11 September 2001, and people paying the price through the loss of their jobs.

Personal success in changing corporate realities

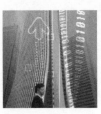

The redefinition of personal success

In the certain world of corporate bureaucratic structures, it was quite easy to measure personal success. Ideas of personal achievement were directly related to positions in organisational hierarchies. These were clearly graded in terms of prestige, pay and fringe benefits. Related to jobs were size of salary, size of office and allocation of parking slot. These somewhat crude job distinctions were further reinforced by preoccupations with detailed status differences. These could range from the quality of carpet on the office floor through to access to catering facilities and corporate hospitality allowances.

The sweeping away of bureaucratic structures is being driven by developments in information technology, demanding customer and citizen expectations and the changing aspirations of employees.

In too many organisations, these features persist. Culture change programmes on both sides of the Atlantic have failed to break them down. All too often, it is the case that these features are superimposed on functional hierarchies relating to the exercise of authority and responsibilities. But organisational realities are rapidly changing. Even in public-sector organisations, most renowned for their rigid hierarchical structures, the break-up of traditional structures is under way. Public and private-sector organisations in France, Germany and southern European countries may still adhere to the bureaucratic model, but in the United States and the United Kingdom, a paradigm shift is under way.

The sweeping away of bureaucratic structures is being driven by developments in information technology, demanding customer and citizen expectations and the changing aspirations of employees. Information technology allows for processes to be monitored through machines rather than by managers. Citizens and consumers expect their needs to be met in personalised ways rather than being treated as an undifferentiated mass. Employees resent being treated as dispensable cogs in bureaucratic machines.

Taken together, these forces have led to the rejection of the bureaucratic model of organisation that, throughout the last century, was held up to be the exemplary model for organisational efficiency. It was not until the last two decades of the twentieth century that it was rejected by more flexible, adaptive, entrepreneurial structures. Today, large companies – the corporate elephants – do everything within their capabilities to behave as entrepreneurial fleas. Small is seen as beautiful and the message to large corporations is to flatten their structures, decentralise their operational and strategic responsibilities, and empower line managers to behave as though they are entrepreneurs running their own businesses.

This has destroyed the underlying mechanisms for motivating corporate managers. In the past, corporate careers were structured in terms of an overriding dream. A dream that was organised around promotion, competing against others and climbing up corporate hierarchies. Sacrifices were made *today* for the rewards to be gained *tomorrow*. Notions of personal self development were determined according to position reached by age attained. The whole mechanism generated corporate commitment and long-term loyalty. This focus was based on the assumption that employees would devote the whole of their working lives to a particular employing corporation that, in return, would offer life-long careers. That is, life-long to the legal age of retirement. These assumptions were further strengthened by practices whereby companies trading in the same sector – financial services were a case in point – would not poach staff from each other.

These stable and predictable careers had broader social ramifications. It produced the Western world's middle classes who occupied the suburbs and the affluent neighbourhoods of the post-war decades. They viewed their futures with optimism as they competed in the corporate race for promotion. Outside work, they could make financial commitments on credit since they knew that their employment prospects were – at the very least – secure but, more likely than not, would allow them to be financially better off tomorrow than they were today.

With corporate restructuring and the adoption of the entrepreneurial paradigm, these features of corporate life have been confined to the dustbins of the past. No longer is life-long employment offered by companies. No longer do they offer secure, predictable career paths. The flattening, break-up and decentralisation of corporate structures and the imposition of entrepreneurial cultures has replaced security with insecurity and certainties with uncertainties.

The outcome is that criteria for personal success are no longer predictable and transparent. A successful career route enjoyed by a 35 year-old male or female high flyer can suddenly be dissipated by a corporate merger or acquisition. After a company take-over, it is not only the potential loss of one's job that creates feelings of vulnerability but also those other ramifications of corporate restructuring. The person who reported to me yesterday is the person to whom, after the merger, I now report today. We are compelled to survive within organisational realities characterised by constant flux in authority relations and operating procedures. In this uncertain world, employees no longer have yardsticks against which they can measure their personal success. With the abolition of job grades, there are no hierarchies to climb. No positions to be achieved within particular age-related time frames. The restless corporation creates the restless employee. Employees who, in their feelings of vulnerability, make token acknowledgments of their corporate commitment, who role-play the excitement they are supposed to gain from their jobs but who are permanently aware that their employment prospects are vulnerable.

In this world of work, employees develop short-term instrumental attitudes towards their employing organisations. They negotiate the best deals that they can in performance-related reward systems. They also develop the appropriate political and interpersonal skills so as not to offend their line managers, superiors and appraisers. Their ideas for changes in operational practices are always guarded and qualified so as not to be interpreted as criticism of existing practices and product portfolios. To do otherwise merely reinforces personal vulnerability in the next job-cutting exercise, whether driven by economic downturn or corporate merger.

Personal success in this uncertain world becomes measured not in terms of careers – that is, not as upward mobility within hierarchical structures – but in terms of material, financial rewards that support material living standards and personal lifestyles for today. Instead of a focus upon present-day sacrifice for corporate rewards in the future, the emphasis is exclusively upon the 'today'. Why not, when the employment relationship is seen to bear such high risks? Why sacrifice 'today' if there are high chances that commitment to the corporation will not or cannot be rewarded in the future?

This attitude leads to high rates of personnel mobility between companies as employees develop transferable skills that allow them to unlock themselves from the clutches of their present

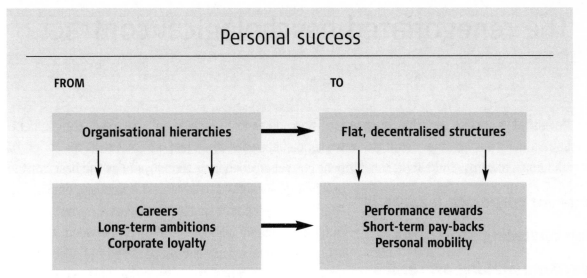

employers. It is a strategy to reduce their vulnerability and dependency upon specific line managers and corporate leaders. But in times when the average occupancy of the CEO's position is around four years, and with constant flux among personnel within and between corporations, what determines criteria of personal success? If corporate positions are so vulnerable and employment prospects so uncertain, it can only be the financial rewards that count. The future can take care of itself and so too, for that matter, can the corporation.

The renegotiated psychological contract

Personal success in the corporate zoo demands intensity of personal commitment. Corporations expect their staff to work wholeheartedly for them but without the offer of traditional rewards. Short-term commitment has superceded long-term loyalty as the basis for the psychological contract between employers and employees. That is the corporate aim. The extent to which this is fulfilled is highly variable, not only between different economic sectors and enterprise size, but also across nations. U.S. companies seem more able to generate employee commitment than their United Kingdom counterparts. This may be the reason for the greater productivity and innovation rates of U.S. companies, particularly in bio-sciences and information and communication technologies.

The challenge for corporate leaders is to develop operating structures, cultures, decision-making processes and leadership styles that explicitly encourage internalised employee commitment.

Essentially, it is possible to separate employees in terms of three types of attitude towards their employment. These may be described as *resentful* and *instrumental compliance* and *internalised commitment.* For high performance, it is the latter that produces the results. The challenge for corporate leaders is to develop operating structures, cultures, decision-making processes and leadership styles that explicitly encourage internalised employee commitment.

Resentful compliance is likely to be short-term. It describes the situation when employees comply with instructions and fulfil their expected tasks in a grudging manner. It was much the feature of large sectors of shop-floor employees in the traditional manufacturing industries in Europe during the greater part of the twentieth century. In these companies, employees worked according to their job descriptions as agreed between management and strong trade unionism. Indeed, trade unionism was both a cause and effect of employees' resentful compliance. It led to the growth of shop-floor organisation, militant trade unionism and, of course, frequent industrial disputes. There was often a high incidence of absenteeism, days off work through minor injuries and illness and, in periods of full employment, high staff turnover. The automobile industries of Europe in the 1960s articulated all of these features. It led to low productivity, poor quality of products, high production costs and, because of these, the ultimate shifting of production by large manufacturers from Europe to the lower cost economies of South-East Asia.

Resentful compliance fosters low trust between employers and employees. Managers operate with the assumption that they know best (and that is why they are in charge) and that employees will do as little as they can get away with. This basic assumption becomes built into the dominant culture of companies with the expectation that their employees are *disengaged*.

This low-trust syndrome leads to excessive bureaucracy, a heavy reliance on rules and high operating costs through the over-use of supervisors and line managers. As staff are not to be trusted, they need detailed job descriptions. As they have detailed job descriptions, employees only do what is asked of them. No more, no less. The results are rigid organisational structures that destroy initiative and innovation. If employees have ideas of how their jobs and company performances can be improved, they keep them to themselves. It is a culture that disempowers and disables rather than empowers and facilitates. By holding back on innovative ideas, managers assume their staff have nothing to contribute. And so they do not consult them. The result is that the low-trust, disengaged culture perpetuates itself with employees continuing to comply with management's instructions but in a resentful manner.

Instrumental compliance is found among employees who regard the employment relationship as entirely contractual and economically grounded. It has nothing to do with emotional engagement but, instead, is steeped in ideas of classical economic theory and the pursuit of economic self-interest. Employees regard the organisation as a pool of resources that can be exploited for personal gain. The salary is simply and solely the tie that holds the two together. Issues of loyalty and commitment are regarded as 'old fashioned', and are replaced by a cash nexus that emphasises performance-related reward systems.

Over the last two decades of the twentieth century, there was a cultural shift from resentful to instrumental compliance. Employees comply and do what is expected of them, so long as they receive financial rewards that they consider to be fair. Corporate values, mission statements, ethical practices etc, are regarded as secondary to this essentially materialistic approach. It encourages employees to ask no questions, to keep their heads down and, of course, not to query or challenge. The outcome is low rates of organisational change and poor performance in product innovation.

Many companies fall into the mistake of believing that by offering high material rewards and deliberately encouraging an instrumental attitude among their employees, this will enhance performance. It may do so in the short-term. It creates a 'buccaneer' culture when everyone, including the managers, are working for the business for their own ends. This is a feature of many high-technology companies. They are structured on the assumption that high material incentives for employees will sustain high corporate performance. But, the reverse is often the case. The culture becomes excessively competitive, with feuding over share-options, bonuses and salary levels. Jealousies break out and conflicting groups appear. Each of these has its own appointed or self-appointed leaders who compete with others to be the strongest baron on the turf. The organisation breaks up into fiefdoms and any shared corporate values are quickly destroyed. To be personally successful in this culture, it is necessary to be politically astute, to align with the appropriate corporate barons and to ensure these are in powerful positions. Only through patronage and mentoring by the powerful barons can personal gains be achieved.

The growing dominance of instrumental compliance among employees accounts for their greater mobility between companies. This is why maintaining personal networks is so important. Through these, personnel get to hear of job vacancies, reward systems and opportunities for buying share-options and gaining performance-related bonuses. A further factor is the nature of 'knowledge' skills. In the old manufacturing economy, the skills of shop-floor employees were tied to their employers' machines. If they were disgruntled, they could hardly walk away. The outcome was employee resentment. With knowledge employees, their skills are more mobile and transferable. This is why financial institutions often have problems in retaining fund managers, software companies their designers and media organisations their 'creatives'. More flexible, mobile labour markets are generating employee attitudes that are more short-term and instrumental.

However, for high innovative performance and longer-term competitive advantage, companies need to cultivate employee attitudes that reflect *internalised psychological commitment*. This is when employees put their hearts and souls into their jobs. They are

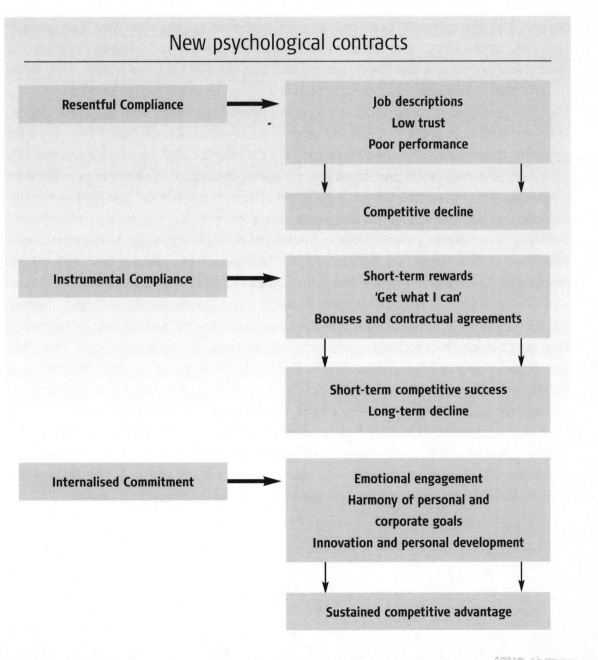

New psychological contracts

Resentful Compliance → Job descriptions
Low trust
Poor performance

↓ ↓

Competitive decline

Instrumental Compliance → Short-term rewards
'Get what I can'
Bonuses and contractual agreements

↓ ↓

Short-term competitive success
Long-term decline

Internalised Commitment → Emotional engagement
Harmony of personal and
corporate goals
Innovation and personal development

↓ ↓

Sustained competitive advantage

committed to the corporate goals and inter-link corporate success with their own personal ambitions. They are fully immersed in the culture of the business and internalise standards of conduct and performance that are in harmony with those of their corporate leaders. They regard the employment relationship as extending beyond a solely instrumental wage contract.

The employment conditions that encourage internalised commitment are fairly atypical. They are found in business start-ups and other entrepreneurial ventures. Small firms are more conducive to generating this than larger companies. Californian high-tech businesses and U.S. companies, in general, seem more capable of generating internalised commitment than European companies, steeped as they are in industrial traditions that generate low trust, employer-employee suspicion and resentful compliance. However, it is the key to high performance. Internalised commitment is likely to lead to innovation, the exploitation and development of new ideas, low costs through a reduced need for supervision, management and detailed job descriptions. The innovative, flexible firm is the outcome of internalised commitment.

The challenge for corporate leaders is to create the appropriate conditions for this. The two-day off-site culture-building activity is unlikely to bear much fruit. It requires heavy investment in employee training and personal professional development, a focus upon open and fluid communication channels and reward systems that allow all employees to regard themselves as stakeholders in the long-term success of their employing companies. The adoption of project-driven management models, with performance-related reward systems can encourage quite the reverse. Their focus on achieving short-term targets can generate an excessive instrumentalism rather than greater employee commitment. Performance-related reward systems on the one hand, and stakeholder share-ownership schemes on the other, may seem closely related. But the differences in their outcomes for employee attitudes and corporate performance could not be greater.

Brains are not enough

For competitive advantage in the knowledge economy, corporations need continuous innovation. The global marketplace forces them to reinvent their product portfolios on an on-going basis. This puts human creativity at the strategic core of the business. Without this, the most sophisticated information systems and Internet technologies will fail to deliver competitive advantage. The capabilities of these technologies are only realised within organisational cultures that encourage the unleashing of human potential through ideas, experimentation and, through these, product development.

The time capabilities of the technologies are only realised within organisational cultures that encourage the unleashing of human potential...

The recognition of this fact by corporate leaders and among policy makers is to emphasise the importance of skills, learning and qualifications. Of course, each of these is important. Far too many companies invest too little in personal training. Most employees are still compelled to 'pick up' the skills needed to do their jobs through informal dialogue with colleagues as well as by a process of ad-hoc self-learning. This is usually the case following internal promotion when employees are more or less left to their own devices to determine how they should do their new jobs.

Even so, an emphasis upon skills and learning is not enough. It merely reinforces the way companies presently do things by maintaining the status quo. In essence, in-house company training leads to conformity and compliance. Existing practices continue and, more often than not, personal creativity is destroyed. If colleagues offer ideas as to how tasks could be undertaken differently or challenge the content of their training programmes, they can easily be labelled as uncooperative and even lacking in organisational commitment.

Equally, a preoccupation with personal qualifications and accreditations is unlikely to nurture corporate creativity. This is particularly so in the modern knowledge economy. In an era when approximately one-half of all young people in Europe and the United States obtain qualifications from universities and other institutions of higher education, these academic awards cannot be used as reliable indicators of personal creativity. What these qualifications reflect is the increasing proportion of young people in modern society who have engaged in an extended period of personal *learning*. This should not be confused with self-development, let alone personal creativity. These graduates have, to varying degrees, assimilated information through attending lectures, reading books and searching the Internet. They have absorbed information so they can be rubber-stamped with credentials. This process has little to do with nurturing personal creativity. It can have quite the reverse effect, as witnessed by those well-known entrepreneurs, artists, authors, inventors etc, who quit college because of the frustrations they experience as part of this learning process. For corporations to promote personal creativity for high innovative performance, it is necessary for them to focus upon promoting employee intelligence. There are three components to this, each of which has to be harnessed if companies are to develop high-performing cultures. There are intellectual, emotional and social dimensions to employee intelligence.

Intellectual intelligence is measured in psychological profiling. Psychologists have countless tests, inventories and other methodologies for calculating personal intelligence 'scores'. On the basis of these, we are regarded as being of 'high', 'above average', 'average' or even 'below average' intelligence. Companies use these in selection procedures and assume they are recruiting the most intelligent and, therefore, 'the best' for their key corporate positions. Those with the highest scores are deemed to be those with the greatest potential for contributing to corporate success. The education systems of the United States and Europe are structured around assumptions about peoples' intellectual intelligence. These are: Intelligence = Intellectual Intelligence = Academic Intelligence = Academic Credentials = Personal Success.

Intellectual intelligence, as measured by tests and inventories, is about the ability to conceptualise. That is, the ability to think in abstract terms. These are the skills of scientists, mathematicians, artists and writers. They are also the skills required in corporations. But it is not enough. They must be combined with emotional intelligence. We are all familiar with young children who have conceptual and imaginary abilities but who lack patience, self-confidence and

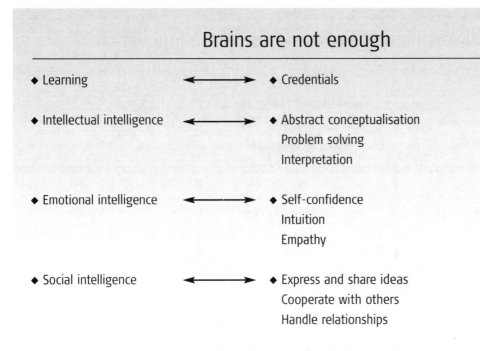

Brains are not enough

◆ Learning	◆ Credentials
◆ Intellectual intelligence	◆ Abstract conceptualisation Problem solving Interpretation
◆ Emotional intelligence	◆ Self-confidence Intuition Empathy
◆ Social intelligence	◆ Express and share ideas Cooperate with others Handle relationships

self-discipline. Equally, we know of colleagues who have great ideas but who quickly become bored with putting them into practice in terms of developing a path-breaking innovative product. The recruitment of personnel on the basis of their intellectual capabilities is insufficient unless this is combined with *emotional intelligence.* Since universities and the higher education systems of the world generally fail to identify and to promote this, it becomes a key task for corporations. But emotional and intellectual capabilities must be combined with *social abilities* if companies are to make full use of their human assets. This requires employees to have the skills to express their ideas and to present their arguments coherently. This requires employees to be able to cooperate with others, to communicate and to motivate. Without these qualities, the insight derived from intellectual intelligence will not be channelled into innovative products and services.

For corporate success, companies have to re-think their assumptions abut personal intelligence. They need to develop the broader definition – to incorporate the social and emotional

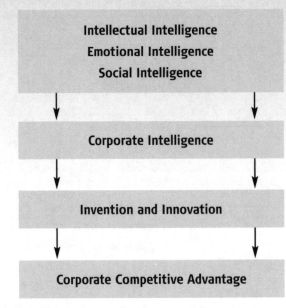

Individual intelligence and corporate innovation

Intellectual Intelligence
Emotional Intelligence
Social Intelligence

Corporate Intelligence

Invention and Innovation

Corporate Competitive Advantage

dimensions. Perhaps they should go even further and throw away their traditional IQ inventories and view their employees through an alternative lens. A perspective that starts from the assumption that the priority should be to recruit those with emotional and social capabilities and that, from these, intellectual intelligence can be enhanced. By encouraging corporate commitment through team dynamics, sociability and open communication flows, cultures can be generated that bring out the best of employees' creativity. For high performance, it is *corporate intelligence* that is needed. This is more likely to be achieved with colleagues who have emotional and social skills rather than those who are only intellectually sharp.

Women as the more intelligent corporate colleagues

In the agrarian systems of pre-industrial Europe, men and women worked within a shared division of labour. Women, as did men, toiled on the land to produce economic surpluses that allowed their family systems to survive. There was little distinction between work and leisure. The two were combined in religious services that celebrated crop yields, harvest time as an occasion for communities to get together, and other such events. Equally, there was little distinction between home and work since the two were more or less the same thing. Family relationships were work relationships, domestic activities were economic production activities and vice versa.

Through their gender-related experiences, women have acquired advantages over men for personal success in future corporations.

Within this network of domestic-based activities, there was a division of labour in terms of what men and women, adults and children were expected to do. Custom and practice defined the nature of these roles such that some activities were deemed suitable as women's work, while others were appropriate for men. With the eighteenth and nineteenth-centuries' industrial revolution, these patterns became transferred to the factory system. Work in the cotton mills in the northern towns of England was considered as suitable employment for women, while the growth of the heavy manufacturing industries such as ship building and steel production created work for men.

With the expansion of heavy manufacturing industries throughout the nineteenth and early twentieth centuries, factory employment became equated with employment for men. A heavy premium was attached to physical strength because of the labour-intensive nature of these industries. The low level of technology of the time meant that much was needed in the form of lifting and moving materials from one place to the next, to say nothing of the long working hours that required high levels of physical stamina. Industrial injuries were rife, as were disabilities and physical exhaustion. State legislation fixed a retirement age in most European countries that was beyond the average life expectancy of industrial workers – around the early to mid-sixties. It was assumed that the cost of pensions to governments would be low since most workers would fail to reach this age. If they did manage to survive, they could not expect to live much longer than retirement age.

As part of this process, women became excluded from large areas of economic activity. They were seen as lacking the physical capabilities needed to work in the rapidly expanding manufacturing sectors of U.S. and European industry. Except during times of national warfare, they were relegated to performing low-paid, routine clerical tasks in offices or in the post-war expanding health, welfare and education systems. Most importantly of all, their primary role was defined to be that of homemaker and manager of the household.

The growth of management, brought about by the emergence of large-scale corporations during the latter part of the twentieth-century, reinforced this pattern. The implementation of management structures and layers of supervision, brought about by the administrative complexities of the large twentieth-century corporation, created career structures for men. Organisation man was born, who in return for his loyalty and commitment, was rewarded by promotion and orderly career progression. In order to fulfil his corporate expectations, it was assumed that corporate man would be married, with a wife who emotionally, socially and administratively 'serviced' him so that he could totally and exclusively focus upon doing good things for the corporation.

End of history lesson. Things have changed. A gender revolution has occurred that has fundamentally altered a wide range of assumptions surrounding male-female relations, to say nothing of domestic and work roles. Education systems have expanded to give equal qualifications to women as to men. Women have developed assertive, self-confident identities with expectations for personal success and reward equivalent to those found among men. Their independent earning capacity allows them to take mortgages so that they can choose to live independently if they wish. This, together with their aspirations for self-fulfilment, allows them continually to evaluate the nature of their 'live-in' personal relationships. If these do not work, they separate. Even the arrival of children ceases to prevent putting the 'me' before the 'other'. This is not to say that women are any more self-focused than men but, simply, that the gender revolution has generated a culture of individualism in which both men and women are encouraged to be assertive and self-confident. Women, to a large degree, have rejected their former subordinate and dependent identities.

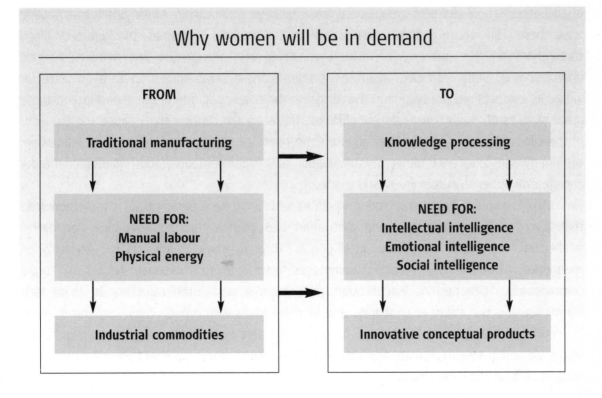

Knowledge-based businesses have continually to change to survive. They have to get the best out of the brains of their staff. This can only be achieved by developing effective team dynamics and interpersonal skills. Cooperation among colleagues working in project teams is at a premium. Leadership styles have to be facilitative in getting ideas from people. Complex issues and challenges have to be managed through problems shared and discussed in open and honest ways. The project-driven corporation places a heavy premium upon tacit understanding among colleagues, empathy and personal intuition. All of these tend to be greater attributes among women than men because of childhood, school and peer-group socialisation processes. Knowledge-based businesses depend upon these skills. These are the research institutes, the media companies, the high-technology corporations and the public-sector institutions coping with the greater and more challenging expectations of better-educated, assertive citizens. In these organisations, there is no place for individual competition, the hoarding of information by colleagues, the one-upmanship and those other features of 'macho' management cultures. These are the cultures that shaped the character of manufacturing corporations. They stressed the need for management rather than leadership; conformity and compliance rather than innovation and experimentation; and organisational order and stability rather than complexity and change.

The knowledge-based corporation operates with a different paradigm. It is a methodology that places a heavy premium upon innovation and change through leveraging employees' intellectual, emotional and social intelligence. Through their gender-related socialisation experiences, women have acquired advantages over men for personal success in future corporations. Their personal socialisation gives them empathy, the capability to share tacit knowledge and the ability to cooperate and to share ideas with others. These are the qualities needed for high performing businesses. Companies neglect them at their peril. So why are there so few women in senior corporate positions today? Why do so few companies fully make use of the creative skills of their employees?

Unregulated rewards in a restless world

What criteria can be used to determine the earnings of those whose productivity cannot precisely be measured? The output of sales people, shop-floor employees and those who produce tangible products can precisely be managed. One of the great management challenges of the twentieth century was to establish the criteria according to which output and performance could be monitored and assessed. The piece-rate systems of the earlier car factories, which then spread to most other spheres of large-scale industrial production, were the extreme expressions of this. They created cadres of time and motion experts, work-study engineers and many others who were paid to calculate the pay of others! The growth

For those of us not selected to become corporate leaders, the best that we can do is to negotiate the best possible rate for the job.

of trade unionism was driven by the desire to obtain fair rewards for rank and file members and this strategy was generally pursued by negotiating 'rates for jobs' that reflected effort required, skills, training and responsibilities.

These systems provided the basis for wage differentials within companies. The outcome was that businesses had hierarchical reward systems, which generally meant that those who were older and had worked for the company for the longest periods of time within the different occupations received the highest wages. A function of this pattern of wage determination was that the majority of employees felt that earning differentials were equitable and fair. There may have been periods of industrial unrest but, on the whole, there was an acceptance that wage rates were locked into patterns of differentials that reflected skills, responsibilities and training.

The advent of the Information Age has blown all these traditional practices out of the window. Most employees perform tasks that cannot easily be measured in relation to explicit criteria of output and performance. Those who work with their brains cannot be subject to the methodologies of work study in the same way as the process workers of the past. From the top to the bottom of the modern organisation, there are no longer any clearly defined criteria according to which employees are rewarded.

How are the salaries of those in senior corporate positions to be determined? Are they generally over or under-paid? Should salaries be linked to the valuation of corporate shares? What is the relevant marketplace for determining their demand? Is there a local, national, regional or even global rate? Or are rewards to be determined in relation to so-called personal skills? How are criteria of leadership, inspiration, energy and all those other qualities that so frequently appear in job advertisements to be quantified and related to remuneration packages? There can be no objective criteria. The outcome is employees who are paid less will constantly query the equity of corporate reward systems and ask whether the people occupying the highest paid jobs really earn their money.

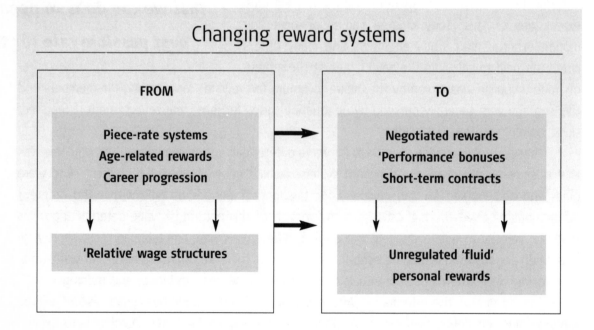

Wage inequalities are increasing in both public and private-sector organisations in many countries in Europe as well as in the United States. These are destroying collective corporate cultures and, with them, employee commitment. Persons appointed to corporate leadership positions many be the most inspirational leaders in the world but, with their lesser-paid colleagues sometimes earning less than twenty-five percent of their salaries, few strategic corporate goals are likely to be achieved if employee motivation is low.

Britain and the United States are becoming very unequal societies. Resentful under-classes are becoming more conspicuous as witnessed by crime rates and urban violence. Reward systems and opportunity structures within companies are becoming more unequal. Those who are in jobs that reward the use of intangible assets (such as brains) are able to command ever-increasing rewards as their performances cannot be measured according to strictly objective criteria. As for the rest, their declining commitment to their companies – surveys show that eighty percent of staff have little or no commitment to their employing organisations – is reflected in low productivity and other inefficiencies. In a knowledge economy, employees do not go on strike.

No chief executive of any company can transform the performance of their businesses alone. To regard them as superhuman celebrities is to create myths that can only hasten their downfall. Witness the fate of recent chief executives at British Airways, Coca-Cola, Disney, Marconi and many other companies. Those appointed to chief executive positions are offered lucrative remuneration packages that PR companies 'spin' to suggest that they reflect global market forces, performance-related reward systems and the intrinsic demands of the job. They rarely spell out the detailed criteria associated with any of these factors. How many CEOs are able to wave job offers in front of corporate head-hunters to support their alleged global demand that justify their high remuneration packages? How far are the details of their jobs spelled out with the same precision as in the piece-rate systems that were applied to measure the productivity and performance of shop-floor employees in manufacturing companies?

We live in a world of myths and short-term instrumental attitudes towards the employment relationship. These infiltrate organisations from top to bottom in both the private and public sectors. It is a fascinating paradox, particularly in view of the resources that organisations devote to staff-training programmes in which they extol the virtues of teamwork, personal commitment and the need to nurture the corporate culture. It is a contradiction that is becoming more transparent as more employees recognise that corporate emperors have no clothes. Perhaps that is why, come their downfall, so many highly paid executives spend the rest of their lives psychologically devastated despite their lucrative exit remuneration packages. They have to accept that they have not only failed but we also know they have conned us. For those of us not selected to become corporate leaders, the best that we can do is to negotiate the best possible rate for the job, recognising that there are no tangible, objective criteria for evaluating our performance in jobs that have precarious, uncertain futures. We get what we can bargain for, using any criteria that will help us to argue our case.

Playing the meritocratic game

Companies continually extol the virtues of fairness and equity of treatment. Legal and cultural changes are compelling them to operate as meritocratic institutions in which there is no place for patronage, favouritism or personal preferment. Legislation insists upon equal opportunities for men and women as well as for those who are members of culturally diverse ethnic, linguistic and national groups. Age discrimination is now outlawed in many countries, reinforcing the trend towards ignoring personal attributes in favour of criteria of personal achievements.

If we want to succeed, we have to be be prepared to accept personal prejudices, preconceived ideas, assumptions and ways of doing things.

These legal changes are being propelled by trends in corporate cultures driven by demographics and the information economy. Knowledge employees have greater expectations of the value of their personal worth. In the pursuit of this, they expect to be fairly treated and assessed in comparison with the contribution of others. The growing numbers of women moving into middle-level corporate leadership positions has been a major force, insisting that their companies implement and adhere to equal-opportunities policies. This is reflected in the political sphere with pressure for legislation to monitor corporate procedures.

But are companies becoming more meritocratic? Undoubtedly, they are more sensitive to the need to become so, and this is reflected in their widespread use of appraisal schemes. What are these if not attempts to evaluate employees in terms of their achievement of prenegotiated targets as well as to assess their personal skill and learning needs? They are intended to bring out the best in colleagues and are usually presented by employing corporations as the major mechanism for assisting staff in their personal development. It all looks good – certainly at face value. Underneath, however, corporate reality may be quite different. For personal success in the modern organisation, it is important to be aware of this 'hidden' reality. The fact is that the shift to devolved, decentralised and more entrepreneurial structures may be making modern corporations *less* rather than *more* meritocratic than their more centralised, bureaucratic predecessors.

Bureaucracies are essentially structured on the basis of rules, regulations and procedures. These determine the parameters of job descriptions, in terms of both what and how tasks are to be achieved. Jobs are hierarchically arranged with clearly defined reporting mechanisms that stipulate duties, responsibilities and accountabilities. Performance and rewards are highly transparent. There is little left for the exercise of personal initiative and discretion. Employees do what is expected of them according to their job descriptions. No more, no less. Equally, they are paid the rate for the job. No more, no less.

It was a German philosopher writing at the beginning of the twentieth century, Max Weber, who stated that bureaucracies were the most efficient forms of administration because of their precisely defined and accountable job descriptions. They were also efficient as organisations because they were fair, with personnel appointed to positions on the basis of their personal qualifications and competencies, rather than by patronage, personal favour and sponsorship. Bureaucracies were essentially meritocratic because criteria of promotion and appointment are explicit in terms of transparent criteria and procedure. There is no place for the exercise of personal discretion.

With the shift to decentralised, post-bureaucratic forms of organisation, the role of personal discretion becomes predominant. In the entrepreneurial corporations, the strategic intent is to create organisational units in which employees are empowered to make decisions and to exercise judgement in order to respond flexibly and rapidly to changes in the business environment. It demands that corporate leaders, as heads of business units, behave as though they are entrepreneurial owner-managers. They are extended autonomy as to how they are to achieve their preset goals through the utilisation of both human and capital resources. The organisational paradigm is exactly the opposite to that upon which bureaucracies are structured. The exercise of personal direction supercedes a dependency upon formal and well- established rules and procedures.

Personnel in entrepreneurial corporate structures are potentially subject to unfair treatment, simply because they are not protected by the explicit rules and job criteria of bureaucracies. In

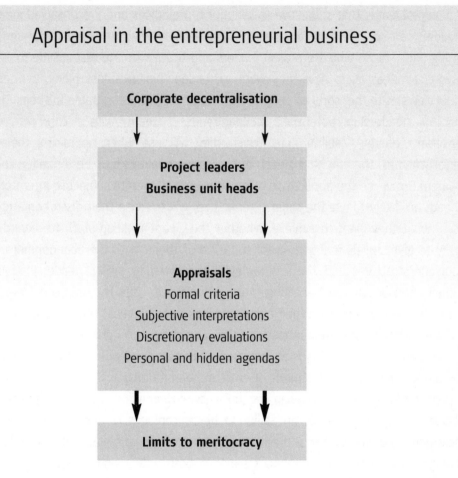

Appraisal in the entrepreneurial business

Corporate decentralisation

Project leaders
Business unit heads

Appraisals
Formal criteria
Subjective interpretations
Discretionary evaluations
Personal and hidden agendas

Limits to meritocracy

other words, their employing organisations are less meritocratic. The counter-claim to this argument is that entrepreneurially structured corporations have in place appraisal and performance-related reward systems. These negate, so it is argued, any potential abuse of authority by business unit leaders and make them equally as meritocratic as bureaucracies, with the added advantage of offering greater opportunities for personal fulfilment through working autonomy and the capabilities for exercising initiative, judgement and decision-making.

The problem is that subjective assumptions, prejudices and preconceived ideas of business unit leaders can become built into personal appraisal systems. Those who manage decentralised operating units, those who are project leaders and those who are responsible for staff appraisal, all have clear ideas as to how they want to pursue their business plans. In these, they have personal views as to the 'sorts of people' they want to have accountable to them. They have clear notions of 'leadership potential', 'colleagueness', 'team skills', 'corporate commitment', 'enthusiasm', 'energy', 'ability', etc, which they will use when appraising their staff. Within appraisal schemes, the criteria for each of the above qualities may be formally explicit and quite transparent. However, the *application* of these criteria is open to subjective interpretation. No two unit heads are likely to use the same criteria. They will exercise their discretion and judgement in terms of what they want to achieve, whether they want to keep staff, to reward and motivate them, or to give signals that they want to be rid of them. With the abandonment of centralised bureaucratic structures and the greater emphasis given to project leadership, patronage and personnel sponsorship are becoming more pronounced. This is reinforced by a tendency for corporate leaders to renege on their responsibilities to employees. They regard HR issues as being part of the duties of operational heads so that employees with grievances have little recourse to central corporate support. This is an outcome of corporate elephants disaggregating themselves to operate as company constellations of entrepreneurial fleas.

Personal success in this changing business environment requires a greater sensitivity to interpersonal skills. It demands an ability to be psychologically flexible with different heads of business units and project teams. It emphasises the need to role-play and to maintain a degree of psychological detachment in order to be mobile both within and between corporations. To be successful in any particular operating unit we need to be sponsored and mentored by our immediate leaders and appraisers. We need to act on our 'leadership skills' according to the criteria used by our appraisers. We have to be able to do this differently and flexibly as we are moved around the organisation and from one project leader to the next. Because of this, and if we want to succeed, we have to be nice to everybody. In other words, we have to be prepared to accept personal prejudices, preconceived ideas, assumptions and ways of doing things. After all, we could be reporting to these people next week. Or, maybe, after the next merger, they could be reporting to us.

The under-use of personal skills

How far do companies fully make use of the skills of their employees? Equally as importantly, how many employees feel that their skills are not being fully utilised by their employers? Most companies seem to suffer from a 'skills imbalance' with employers and employees failing to see eye-to-eye on this matter. In periods of growth, corporate leaders will be arguing that skills shortages are holding the company back at the same time as their staff are complaining about their under-promotion and the boring, tedious nature of their jobs, which offer them little opportunity for personal development.

Personal skills are not derived from formal qualifications but from working in conjunction with others.

The major factor that accounts for this state of affairs is rigid mindsets, particularly within the HR, personnel and training departments of large companies. This is a legacy of scientific management in terms of how these principles were applied in manufacturing companies throughout the twentieth century. According to this approach, jobs could be structured to determine the 'one best way' of doing things. On this basis, it was possible to determine the skill needs and the training required to do these jobs. The outcome was to stipulate explicit criteria, which determined the content and the demarcation of individuals' training requirements. There was an almost total emphasis upon formal qualifications, both academic and vocational.

During the twentieth century, the application of the principles of scientific management created rigid, even caste-type, corporate structures. It became more difficult for employees to work their way up from the shop floor and to move into supervisory and managerial positions. Corporate knowledge and long-term practical experience were relegated, to be considered as of secondary importance to the possession of credentials and formal qualifications. Somehow, attending university or college for three years, studying history, ancient classics and drama was deemed to be more relevant than twenty years working on the company's shop floor. The former experience was seen as creating leadership potential in ways in which working for the company did not.

Scientific management brought about the bureaucratisation of management as work-study engineers, management consultants and cost accountants observed, counted and measured how managerial tasks were undertaken. The consequent delineation of job descriptions and the specification of the formal educational qualifications needed to perform these jobs were the key corporate drivers for the expansion of higher education in both the United States and Europe. It was the duty of educational systems to produce graduates with qualifications so that they could be 'slotted' into corporate hierarchies. This reinforced the caste-like character of major companies as they increasingly turned to state-sponsored education systems to meet their skill needs and their HR requirements. This has imposed inflated expectations upon universities, colleges and schools to produce not only graduates with 'knowledge' and 'education' but also specific training that can be exploited directly by employing corporations.

At first glance, these developments would suggest a shift towards the meritocratic organisation. People are appointed to their jobs according to their formal qualifications. The reality is quite the opposite. Education systems can never meet the specific training needs of large corporations. It is impossible for them to produce graduates who can slot neatly into corporate positions. Generalised education and specific training for particular jobs are quite separate and distinct activities. To regard the two as the same is to sustain the myths that allow companies to blame governments and universities for their own skill shortages. It is a strategy that allows companies to renege on their own training obligations to their employees. It is an attempt to justify low spend on what, in an information age, should be a major corporate responsibility. It leads companies to neglect on-the-job training and the general enhancement of skills within their own particular business contexts.

Equally, an over-emphasis upon formal qualifications mitigates against the meritocratic organisation because it devalues the knowledge, experience and skills of those who do not have these credentials. It assumes they lack potential for both promotion and personal skills enhancement. In other words, it leads to the gross under-utilisation of personal talents. It also allows corporate leaders to claim there are skill shortages for which they are not responsible. It means that large numbers of employees are excluded from corporate career structures, to be confined to boring, low-skill, low-paid jobs. They become typecast as unsuitable for promotion. So much for the meritocratic corporation.

It is now many decades since management theorists argued the need for job enrichment and employee empowerment. Despite the massive expansion of MBA programmes and executive education, managers still seem not to have learned some of these key messages. Today, on-the-job training is neglected, while job descriptions, in too many organisations, seem to be cast in stone. Rigid mind-sets prevail and skill shortages appear every time there is economic upturn.

In the high-performing corporation, different cultures prevail. In these, the starting assumption is that all employees have potential and it is the responsibility of corporations to realise this in order to enhance both personal and business success. In flexible, adaptive organisations, there are no job descriptions and the principles of scientific management are rejected. Recruitment into the organisation is through mechanisms that assess generalised employment potential in terms of individuals' possession of not only intellectual but also social and emotional abilities. The HR strategy in high-performing businesses is to regard employees as individuals with 'holistic' capabilities and not merely the possessors of specific skills that can be developed in relation to the performance of particular jobs.

The principles of project management and the reconstitution of companies on the basis of decentralised operating units demand the exercise of flexible, holistic skills. They also require individuals with expertise and detailed competencies. However, unlike working in bureaucracies, these skills develop out of team dynamics. By working in collaboration with colleagues, each develops their own particular abilities and skills. Each becomes dependent upon the other for developing his or her own personal competencies. It is as though each member of the project team or business unit is a musician in an orchestra. Without both the conductor and the other specialist musicians, each is unable to perform and develop their own particular abilities. Soccer and baseball players encounter similar experiences.

What is also interesting about orchestras and sports teams is that high performance cannot be purchased in the marketplace. Soccer and baseball coaches pay huge sums to players who have

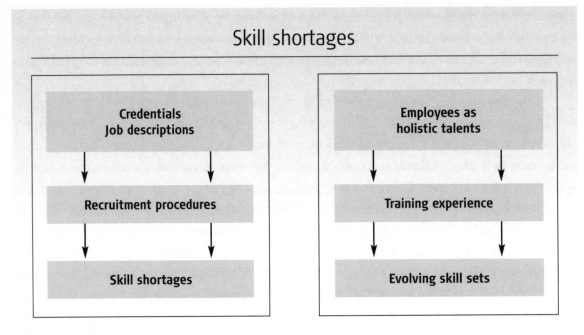

Skill shortages

demonstrated, through their track record with other clubs, that they have the *potential* to perform. But this *potential* is only realised on the basis of 'on-the-job' training with other players in the team. If the coaching is poor and training ineffective, the signed-up player will under-perform. To be successful with the new club, the player has to learn to cooperate with the other team members in order to understand their tactics and to develop empathy and shared understanding. In other words to acquire tacit knowledge. That is why so many soccer and baseball teams fail even when they have spent large sums on several star players. The coaching regimes fail to develop shared understanding of each player's strengths and weaknesses. The quick fix does not work.

And so it is in the corporate world. The overemphasis upon formal qualifications in recruitment processes does not always lead to high performance. Quite the reverse. It can lead to the under-utilisation of personal skills and the under-development of personal talents of those already working in the corporation. Most importantly, it fails to recognise that personal skills are not derived from formal qualifications but from working in conjunction with others. It is in this way that tacit knowledge is acquired and, in the final analysis, corporate performance is dependent upon this. This knowledge cannot be acquired in business schools, examined with qualifications awarded. It can only be obtained through on-the-job training, coaching and working with others through a process of continuous mutual adjustment. This is what separates high-performing sports teams from the average. It is also why, in high-performing companies, the absence of job descriptions and excessive bureaucratisation reduces the level of skill shortages.

For personal success in an uncertain corporate world, what do employees need from their employing companies? Essentially, employees require on-the-job training and continuous professional development. Collapse these elements together and there is the acquisition of tacit knowledge. Knowledge that can be used in a variety of corporate settings as individuals pursue employment strategies that are located within broader economic sectors rather than within specific corporate contexts. Each corporate employer is 'used' to acquire greater experiences and insights that can be exploited for personal advancement. In this way, inter-corporate mobility enhances not only our intellectual but also our social and emotional skills. Again, the analogy with baseball and soccer stars springs to mind. However, we always need to be nice to our project leaders. Our relationship with each of them may be temporary, but we still need their personal endorsement to get the next job.

The entrepreneurial alternative

There is an alternative to competing in the corporate zoo. It is to set up our own businesses. Instead of reporting to project leaders and heads of business units who are forced to take on the entrepreneurial mantle, why not become entrepreneurs ourselves? This is a question increasing numbers of knowledge employees are asking themselves.

The economies of Europe and the United States all have thriving economic sectors dominated by ethnic entrepreneurs

In an information age, business start-up is far easier than opening a manufacturing enterprise. The capital requirement is lower, and the risks associated with failure can be written off more easily. For those working with their brains, the only capital assets needed to start an entrepreneurial venture are a modem, study space and headed paper for invoicing clients. All the other required skills are derived from knowledge and personal networks with potential customers and business partners. These features are most apparent in media industries such as advertising, public relations, journalism and even television production. They are also evident in financial services, management consultancy, marketing and selling, and educational and administrative services.

The most important asset in business start-up in the twenty-first century is customer knowledge. From an understanding of this, services can be provided, added value generated and profits made. If the sale of services entails manufactured goods, the production of these can be outsourced to lower cost producers. The same applies to the distribution and storage of tangible products. With local, national, regional and global supply chains, enabled by the communications revolution, small businesses can trade as global operations. In this sense, many entrepreneurial ventures – derived from customer knowledge – can be considered as the 'consolidators' of goods and services. That is to say, their prime function is to integrate a range of diverse activities into products and services that meet clients' needs. Many entrepreneurial ventures in the Information Age are the embodiment of so-called network or virtual organisations.

Equally, small entrepreneurial ventures are able to market and sell their products in the global marketplace. They are no longer confined to doing business in restricted geographical localities. The Internet allows the knowledge of their products and services to be disseminated around the world and for purchasing transactions to take place. Witness how quickly small farmers in France have embraced Internet technologies to market and sell holidays in their rural cottages, and how craft workers in India have formed consortia to promote their artefacts as Christmas gifts to U.S. and European customers.

If the communications revolution has reconfigured global markets and provided far greater opportunities for the setting up of entrepreneurial ventures so, too, has the changing culture of consumers. No longer do they wish to be treated as undifferentiated masses. The days are gone when they had aspirations for conformity in their lifestyles and purchasing patterns. Today, consumers want 'to be different'. They purchase products and services in order to express their individuality and the uniqueness of their personalities. This means that consumer markets have become fragmented into specialist market niches. Meeting these more focused consumer needs gives small firms greater competitive advantage over their larger counterparts. It offers them business opportunities. At the same time, entrepreneurs' strategic foresight into how these more focused consumer needs are likely to develop in the future can be the basis for entrepreneurial ventures.

So why continue to be employed in large corporations? Particularly in view of the uncertainties associated with continuous corporate restructuring, mergers and acquisitions and, not least, the everyday disagreements with line managers, appraisers, project leaders and business unit managers? If working in large companies has now become so insecure, why not sell personal skills in the marketplace rather than to employers? Why not substitute the employment relationship with a market relationship? Many employees are choosing this option. There is the 'pull' of recognising that the risks of business start-up are lower than they used to be and that the opportunities for making money are greater. There is the 'push' associated with the insecurities and stresses of working in decentralised, fragmented project-driven corporations.

The setting up of entrepreneurial ventures is increasing among four categories of people. These are the young; the redundant and early retired; women; and ethnic/national minorities. One of the major legacies of the dot.com boom (and bust) was that it offered a role model to young people of 'what could be done'. It demolished for good the idea that entrepreneurship and business management were the exclusive preserve of older men. It offered new role models of business proprietorship and presented the flexibility of an alternative career path to that of working in the large corporation. The experience of higher education encourages young people to value their personal autonomy. It also nurtures attitudes that challenge authority and the status quo. The outcome is a cynicism towards the employment relationship and a reluctance to be accountable to others. An increasing number of young graduates view employment in large organisations as a temporary stepping stone. Now, this is endured for the purposes of gaining experience, acquiring tacit knowledge and enhancing their emotional and social skills. Once these assets are acquired, they quit their jobs and set up their own entrepreneurial ventures.

The early retired and those made redundant are also more likely to start up their own businesses. Ageism in large corporations is rife, particularly in Europe where equal opportunities legislation is not fully enforced. After a corporate merger or a cost-reduction campaign, older employees are often the first to lose their jobs. Corporations under-value the skills and experiences acquired by these employees. The paradox is that this leads to a corporate waste of talent as witnessed by those who, regarded by their companies as redundant and dispensable, proceed to set up their own successful business ventures. Exploiting their personal skills and utilising personal networks they have built up as employees, they are able to establish successful business operations.

The growing number of women who quit their corporate positions to start-up their own ventures is further testimony to the inability of large corporations to utilise fully human talents. Despite their greater interpersonal skills, their ability to work in teams and to share ideas with colleagues, women are still passed over for promotion. They are often perceived to be technically competent within various functional areas of expertise but are seen to lack the operational qualities needed for project leadership and appointment to senior corporate positions. This is a result of men promoting in terms of their own image. The gender glass ceiling may have been removed at the operational levels of corporate activity but it still persists in relation to senior strategic positions. This will change over the coming decades as the social and emotional attributes of women are seen as making exceptional contributions to corporate innovation and, therefore, competitive advantage. But, in the meantime, the alternative for aspiring corporate women is either to grin and bear it or to quit and set up their own entrepreneurial ventures. Increasing numbers in the United States and Europe are choosing this option. In this, they are demonstrating their exceptional qualities as entrepreneurs through having higher growth rates and a lower incidence of start-up failure than men in similar economic sectors.

The exclusion from mainstream corporate life is particularly experienced by men and women from ethnic and national minority backgrounds. Notwithstanding equal opportunities legislation and the attainment of comparable educational qualifications, they remain under-represented in senior corporate positions. There are improvements but these are not fast enough to satisfy the aspirations of young people. Their increasing frustrations are expressed by either accepting things as they are, fighting for change or by starting their own businesses. The economies of Europe and the United States all have thriving economic sectors dominated by ethnic entrepreneurs. These people have identified changing consumer needs and, with astute business acumen, responded to these by setting up highly profitable ventures.

Attractions of entrepreneurship

- Autonomy and personal control
- Use of personal creative talents
- Overcoming barriers to personal development in large organisations
- Overcoming prejudice and corporate mindsets experienced among:
  - Women
  - Older men
  - Ethnic/national minorities

Each of these separate and distinct groups is attracted to entrepreneurship through a range of push and pull factors. But this happens within the context of an overall culture change, characteristic of the Information Age. It is a culture change enabled by the growth of business opportunities where intellectual capital and personal qualities are key assets rather than machinery and technical equipment. It is also a cultural change generated by the structural shifts of large corporations. The ever-changing corporation, constantly vulnerable to merger and acquisition, operating in a restless global environment, creates personal insecurities and uncertainties. The post-bureaucratic paradigm, with corporations functioning as decentralised, fragmented operating structures with project management as their key organising principle, reinforces these vulnerabilities. The need to work with colleagues, to be directly accountable to project leaders and line managers and to be rewarded according to transparent performance measures adds further. So why not escape from the corporate zoo? It is a choice that more of us are making. At least then we are only answerable to ourselves.

Organising disorganisation: Life in the reinvented corporation

The Americanisation of management

Managing cultural diversity is now a core component of most MBA programmes. Gone are the days when there was an assumption that the American model of business could effectively be implemented in all national environments. The growth of Japanese corporations in the 1960s and 1970s reminded us that there were ways of doing business other than those methods taught to us by Harvard professors and U.S.-based management consultants. In fact, the cultural limits of the American model have more recently been confirmed by developments in Russia and Central Europe.

The demands and stresses of operating according to the Anglo-American model of organisation seems to be leading to an increasing rate of personnel burn-out.

However, Britain is more accepting of the American model of management than most other countries. It is the adoption of this that leads many U.S. and British managers to fail to understand how business practices are fundamentally different in the rest of Europe. The outcome is that many mergers and acquisitions, strategic alliances and joint ventures with European companies do not achieve their intended objectives. A merger or joint venture may make sense from a hard-nosed strategic point of view, but differences in working practices often prevent these goals from being achieved. So what are some of the major differences between the Anglo-American model of management and those found in many other countries in Europe?

Essentially, U.S. and British companies are structured on the principles of project management. In the 1980s, companies were downsized, with tiers of management eliminated. In the 1990s, management fashion embraced the ideas of business process re-engineering so that organisations were broken down into customer-focused trading units. Sometimes these were established as subsidiary companies while in other cases they were set up as profit-making trading units, profit and loss and cost centres. During the 1990s, these principles were applied as vigorously to public-sector organisations in Britain as they were to private-sector corporations. Hospitals, schools, universities, social-service departments, as well as large sectors of national government, now operate on the basis of project-management principles that have built into them operational targets, key success factors and performance-related reward systems.

The underlying objectives for this widespread process of organisational restructuring were to increase the transparency of operational practices, to encourage personal accountability, to gain efficiencies in client or customer service delivery and to relate rewards directly to performance.

All of this established a management culture that is entrepreneurial and focuses almost entirely upon the short term. It also created highly segmented organisational structures since the incentives and rewards that employees gain are entirely related to the activities of their own particular operating units. This business model has also required the development of new personal skills. We are now encouraged to be leaders instead of managers by setting goals and incentive systems for our staff. We have to be cooperative team members rather than work in a more isolated fashion. We have to accept that, in these highly flattened and decentralised organisational structures, there are very limited career prospects. We are to be motivated by target-related rewards rather than a longer term commitment to our employing organisations as a whole.

This is in sharp contrast to the model of management that operates in the rest of Europe. The principles of business process re-engineering have never been fully accepted in France, Germany and the other major economies. In Russia, the attempt to apply these during the 1990s virtually brought the entire economy to its knees and created huge business opportunities for corrupt middle managers and others who quickly became associated with Mafia business ventures. They could not believe their luck when, through applying U.S. management consultancy advice, they were allocated financial resources and given operational autonomy to manage these in newly-created stand-alone business units. Corporations in the developed economies of Europe have continued to adhere to the bureaucratic model that delivered economic growth for them throughout the twentieth century. European corporations continue to be structured on the basis of hierarchical management principles, with clearly defined job descriptions and explicit channels of reporting. Decision making, although incorporating consultative processes, remains essentially top-down.

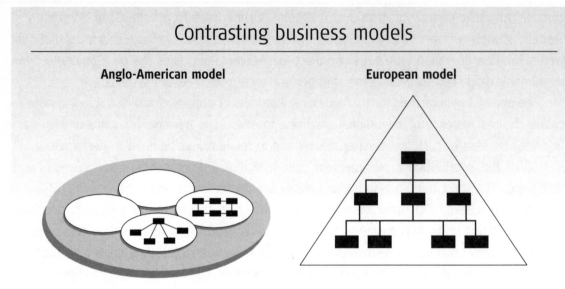

Contrasting business models

Anglo-American model   **European model**

So what are the outcomes and which of these two models is preferable? Certainly, the downside of the Anglo-American model is now becoming evident. The application of the principles of decentralised project management has generated a culture of long working hours. Whether it is in a hospital, a software company or a factory, the breakdown of work processes into project-driven targets inevitably leads to underestimates of the resources needed. It often leads to the unrealistic discounting of the unforeseen problems that are likely to arise. The result is that the success of projects often demands excessively long working hours for the targets to be achieved.

A further outcome is that the criteria of success, in terms of performance targets, are inevitably arbitrary and the source of ongoing dispute. Witness how British teachers and medics refute the validity of the performance measures that have been applied to them by successive governments. Equally, there are inherent ambiguities in performance-related reward systems. In a factory producing automobiles, the output of individuals is directly measurable but what criteria can be used to measure the output and performance of employees in knowledge-based activities such as R & D centres, government offices and even marketing departments of large corporations?

The demands and stresses of operating according to the Anglo-American model of organisation with its re-engineered, decentralised business units seem to be leading to an increasing rate of personnel burn-out. Is it surprising that we queue up to take early retirement? Could this be why labour-market participation rates have declined so significantly for those in the fifty-year-old age group in Britain during the 1980s and 1990s? There are other reasons for retirement in the countries of mainland Europe.

By contrast, the European management model allows for family-friendly employment policies and working hours directives to be implemented. It encourages staff to have a longer term psychological commitment to their employing organisations since they can assume they have longer term employment opportunities with available career prospects. On the other hand, companies operating on the basis of target-focused project management principles may be committed to family-friendly employment policies. But, if the business plan has to be prepared by the end of the month, the advertising campaign completed by the end of next week and the throughput of patients to achieve certain measurable targets, are we really going to let our 'team' down by 'clocking off' at 5 pm and taking our full entitlement of annual leave? Perhaps this is why the French and the Italians are so admired for their quality of life.

Self-managed structures and the split-personality corporation

Contradictory forces are shaping organisational structures. On the one hand, there is a loosening of management processes. At the same time, there is a tightening of controls. The outcome is the split-personality company, often riddled with tensions, conflicts and personal insecurities. How is this happening?

In the split-personality corporation, there is constant oscillation between the forces of centralisation and decentralisation.

In the past, companies operated as neat machines. Jobs were clearly defined in terms of pay, duties and responsibilities. We were told what to do and how to do it. This model was ideal for the manufacturing company. It is totally irrelevant for the knowledge-based business of today. That is, companies where brainpower is the major capital asset. In a marketplace that is constantly changing, companies have continually to reinvent themselves through developing new products and services. Product lifecycles are reducing and profit margins tightening. More competitive global, regional and national business environments compel organisations to be fast. It means they have to develop highly adaptive processes. Corporate flexibility is replacing corporate stability. This places a high premium on employees being inventive, resourceful and continually adapting their work roles owing to ever-changing work expectations.

In these organisational contexts, employees need to be 'left alone'. They have to be given greater operational autonomy with increased levels of authority and responsibility. Many employees do not want this. And why should they if these additional demands are not recognised in performance-appraisal schemes and reward systems? Even so, in high-performing competitive businesses, employees have to be empowered to make day-to-day decisions. Decisions for

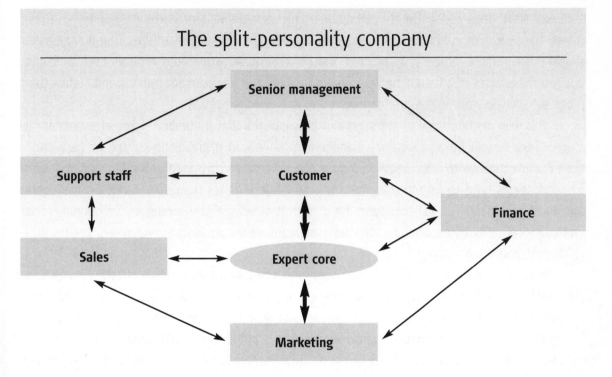

The split-personality company

product development, clinching sales deals and agreeing clients' marketing budgets have to be taken quickly if revenues and sales projects are not to be lost.

It is this trend that is loosening up corporate structures. It is rendering obsolete the dominant management styles of the twentieth century. The days of the autocratic hierarchically focused manager are numbered. Companies are having to take seriously, rather than pay lip-service to, issues of employee empowerment. This is forcing them to look at different models of management. Instead of looking for inspiration to the ideas of The Ford Motor Company and traditional manufacturing, they are having to turn their attention to traditional professional practices, research institutions and even universities. Many companies, both large and small, have already put such methodologies in place. Leading-edge companies in the pharmaceutical, high-technology and media industries are doing this. With their highly qualified professional and technical staff, they recognise that traditional line management practices do not work. These offend the psychological make-up of employees and inhibit innovative cultures. The outcome is a simple management process. A process that is essentially structured around time and cost budgets. These are negotiated between team leaders and senior management and, other than progress reviews, work teams are empowered to achieve their results.

This new methodology of management presupposes that a number of key elements are in place. There has to be a delegatory management style and a prevailing culture of high trust. Reward systems have to encourage employee commitment to corporate goals. Those responsible for work teams have to be effective, inspirational leaders rather than drab hands-on managers. But, most importantly of all, employees have to be trained with the necessary emotional, social and technical skills to be able to take self-confident decisions within parameters set by their colleagues and team leaders.

However, the loosening of corporate structures through the application of self-management principles is being paralleled by the tightening up of processes. This is the other side of the split-personality of twenty-first century companies. Alongside extended operating autonomy, key success factors and performance indicators are being put in place. We may be given greater autonomy in terms of *how* we achieve out goals but *what* we achieve is now subject to far greater measurement, scrutiny and accountability. Those who, in the past, enjoyed working autonomy in terms of both *how* and *what* they did are now subject to measures that make their performance

Organisational principles

- ◆ Small decentralised operating units
  - *Projects/trading units*
- ◆ Strategic devolution
- ◆ Maintenance of flexible terms
- ◆ Team leadership
- ◆ Tight central management control through financial budgets, time budgets and business plans

far more transparent. And they do not like it. This is not just among R & D personnel in private-sector companies but witness the resentment among teachers, academics, medics, social workers and the many others whose outputs are now subject to performance reviews. There is constant protest over the reliability and validity of these measures being used to assess performance and the rewards that are offered as a result.

These conflicts can destroy the commitment of personnel to their employing organisations. But the split-personality corporation is also riddled with other tensions. Many of these are related to the parameters of self-management. What are work teams really responsible for? What authority do they have for decision-making without referral to higher levels of management? This is usually a source of ambiguity such that team leaders will complain that their 'bosses' are being heavy handed and failing to delegate to them while, at the same time, the bosses criticise the team leaders for failing to exercise their delegated authority.

These tensions are never fully resolved. In the split-personality corporation, there is constant oscillation between the forces of centralisation and decentralisation. When businesses are doing well, managers loosen up their structures and encourage employee empowerment. When things are not so good, they tighten up. This is probably quite the reverse to what is really needed in periods of economic recession. These are the times when the self-confidence of senior management is truly tested. Unfortunately, too many fail the test.

From management to leadership

We are often told that there are too many managers in the world but not enough leaders. But is there any difference? Perhaps the contrasts can best be illustrated by comparing the operation of two separate business units. For the sake of corporate confidentiality, let us call them units A and B.

Excessive corporate decentralisation with the abuse of authority by managers can drive many talented people out of the business...

Both trade in similar products and both are wholly owned subsidiaries of larger companies. Each of these parent businesses has an annual turnover of roughly $10 million and the operating units account for about five percent of this. Each employs some forty people with a core staff of about twenty-five, the rest being administrative. The financial survival of both business units is dependent upon the creative talents of their core staff.

Despite these similarities, the differences between these two business units could not be greater. Business unit A has high productivity and a tradition of innovation. It is well known in the industry and highly regarded by employers and employees. It attracts high quality staff when vacancies arise but these are rare because labour turnover is so low. It has a reputation for the quality of its products. Its chief executive officer often speaks at business forums to explain the success of the company.

Although set up at about the same time, ten years ago, the experiences of unit B could not be more different. It has had three chief executives during this period (with a fourth soon to be appointed), a reputation for mediocre products and low staff morale. Labour turnover is high, so is the rate of absenteeism. The staff work long hours and do as they are told. Whereas those employees in unit A seem to regard their work as fun, those in B treat it as drudgery. Needless to say, there is little in the form of either creativity or product innovation. If unit A is admired in the industry, unit B is known as a poor place to work.

But, according to the management textbooks, unit A has got it entirely wrong while B has got it absolutely right. In B there is a strong preference for line-management practices and for operational specification. The CEO rarely consults his staff but, instead, issues instructions. He has established a number of committees through which he manages the business unit. The emphasis is upon hierarchy, procedure and protocol. In short, the business operates as a well-oiled machine. It would make an excellent case study for a discussion of F.W. Taylor and the principles of scientific management. In many ways, the CEO personally embodies these ideals by wearing a suit and by his utter discomfort in engaging in informal discourse with his colleagues.

Unit A, however, would seem to be a nightmare for any case study of organisational best practice. The word most outsiders would use to describe its operating procedures is chaos. The CEO walks around in an open-neck shirt that often hangs out of his trousers. This sums up his management style which, is high on informality. He regards his staff as fellow colleagues and as

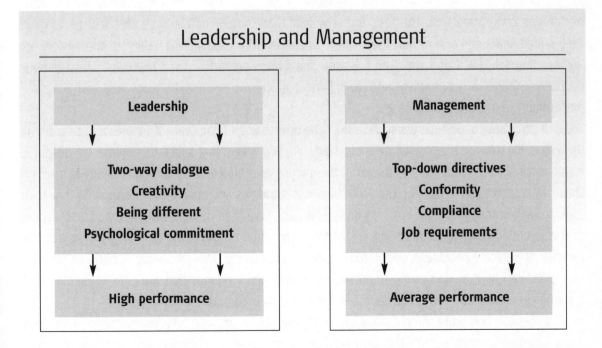

Leadership and Management

Leadership
Two-way dialogue
Creativity
Being different
Psychological commitment
High performance

Management
Top-down directives
Conformity
Compliance
Job requirements
Average performance

equals. There are few formal meetings and decisions are taken informally and with broad consultation. There is a high level of sociability among staff outside working hours. Unit A operates according to entirely contrasting assumptions and principles to those of unit B. The CEO would hardly impress the headhunters whereas his conventionally dressed colleague in unit B is the epitome of good, solid business practice. And, yet, his business unit is under performing, while unit A is delivering returns above the sector average.

What does a comparison of two such similar businesses tell us about management? One, perhaps, is never to appoint accountants as CEOs (as in unit B)! They generally lack the flair and the imagination to motivate staff. But, perhaps, the more important lesson is that, in an information-based business in which survival is dependent on product innovation and the creativity of staff, the prime necessity is for leadership rather than management.

Unit A has effective leadership and, whereas creative staff will respond to this, they will resent bitterly the imposition of management. It is this that differentiates so many high-performing companies from the rest. But why is it that companies continue to put their faith in grey-suited management rather than often unconventional leadership? Why is the history of Richard Branson, Bill Gates and Larry Ellason the exception rather than the rule? Management nurtures cultures of conformity and compliance, quite the reverse features required of high-performing, fast-moving businesses.

It can, though, be even worse than this. The downsizing of corporate structures and their break up into semi-autonomous operating units have allowed many managers to operate as despotic, hierarchically focused little Hitlers. These are the managers empowered by corporate heads to manage their own budgets and to develop their own business strategies and operational practices. In this, they are encouraged to regard their business units as if they were their own personal assets. The outcome of this extended operational autonomy is that there can often be the abuse of managerial power, the exercise of personal patronage and a dominance of subjectivity over rationality in decision-making. One effect can be that women, for example, are overlooked for promotion since their male head of units perceive their non-work obligations as restricting their corporate commitment.

Excessive corporate decentralisation, with the abuse of authority by managers, can drive many talented people out of the business, as is the case in business unit B. It seems that corporate restructuring is allowing corporate leaders to renege on their responsibilities to employees. Corporate leaders in these structures are able to abdicate their broader employee obligations and responsibilities and claim these to be matters for heads of units. The result is that employees' commitment and trust are destroyed, together with their innovation and creativity. If companies are to develop highly devolved, decentralised operating structures, they must place a greater need on developing leadership skills at both the senior corporate level as well as within each of the separate developed operating units.

Managers in the future – temporary but permanent

Interim management – the use of agency-based or freelance managers on a short-term basis - has recently experienced rapid growth and we can expect this to continue. The corporate change of the 1990s will be exceeded by the business transformations of the coming years. The predictable careers of managers are becoming confined to the litter-bin of the twentieth century. The average life of a business before it is sold, merged or taken over is now six or seven years. The job tenure of CEOs is now down to three or four years, while the company tenure of managers is around seven.

If companies want to capture the highest calibre talent, they will have no choice but to draw more heavily on the services of interim management services.

The unprecedented challenges facing companies require them to be continuously innovative, imaginative and strategically flexible. This applies to all aspects of their operations, ranging from product and service delivery to human resource management. This demands that management is always fresh, fit and fun. There is no way that management teams can possess, on a permanent basis, the skills that a company needs to face up to its ever-changing challenges.

This means that management teams must be continually renewed. At one moment, there is the need to launch a new product, at another to 'right size' an operating unit, at yet another to manage an acquisition. Each of these requires very different management skills, which neither permanent managers nor management consultants may be able to provide. As a result, the role of the interim manager is becoming indispensable to corporate success in the future. If, today, interim management makes up a minority of corporate management positions, in the future it will be very much the majority. Interim managers are likely to constitute the leadership core of the future organisation.

Businesses of the future may be considered as either elephants or fleas. Interim managers will be vital for the survival of both. The elephants will be those large global corporations that will continue to dominate supply chains in the production, distribution and sale of manufactured goods and services. But they will function more as virtual companies. They will not own manufacturing, distribution and selling facilities. Essentially, their core competencies will be based on customer knowledge, product development, marketing, promotion and design. In other words, they will be little more than experts in brand management. This is already the case with companies such as Nike and Benetton and it is rapidly becoming the aspiration of major global manufacturers such as Ford and Unilever.

As these elephants face new challenges, they will also need to reinvent their management teams. It is only through the continuous renewal of skills, talent and knowledge that these companies will be able to survive. By their very nature, elephants are not nimble and, yet, markets are permanently changing. The resolution of this dilemma lies in interim management. De facto, this is already becoming common practice with the high turnover of management teams.

Unfortunately, this causes more problems than it solves. What happens is that managers are hired on the promise of careers and long-term prospects but they find a reality that is quite different. Inflated expectations remain unfulfilled and, after a while, it becomes clear that the manager in fact lacks the skills that the business needs in a changing situation. Very few managers are sufficiently skilled and adaptable to respond to the changing needs of companies over time. To hire a manager to tackle a particular challenge may be fine, but what happens when that problem is solved? In the old days, companies could cope by using the talents built within their permanent management structures. But, in an era of rapidly shortening product lifecycles and increasing global competition, this is no longer enough. Continuous management renewal is becoming an essential requirement in the high-performing business model. Interim management will become the rule – not the exception.

This will force companies to rethink the basis of their corporate cultures. How will they manage ever-changing management teams? How will they generate commitment and engagement among strategically indispensable staff who nevertheless regard their tenure in the businesses as fixed and short term? What incentives can be used to substitute for careers, promotion and share-options? This is a major challenge for the elephants of the future. The solution undoubtedly rests in them developing long-term strategic partnerships with service providers similar to those they have built with component suppliers and so on.

The next few years will witness the growth of interim management companies acting as specialist service providers, working in collaboration with their client companies on a long-term basis. In this way, they will develop a detailed and in-depth understanding of their clients' business needs as these emerge and transform. The relationship will require service providers to understand their clients' corporate cultures, their ways of doing things, their strategic agendas, their business plans and, most importantly, the dynamics of their management processes. Only then can the appropriate interim managers be provided. This, of course, demands the nurturing of deep and trusting relationships, which can only be developed in the long term and built on a deep understanding of one another's business practices.

In the future, this will lead to increasing specialisation among interim management companies. Each will develop specific skills in relation to the particular needs of different client companies, industries and business sectors. In this, their branding strategies of different client companies, industries and business sectors will be vital if they are to gain market share and not simply be providers of management skills. They will need to take on a more proactive role in marketing themselves to client companies as well as attracting high-calibre talent that can excel at the interim manager's demanding role. It will no longer be enough to have a database of potential managers who are allocated to client companies. Such reactive strategies will be inadequate for meeting the heightened expectations of corporations who use interim managers

Interim management

Needed for:

◆ Corporate re-invention
◆ Drastic corporate restructuring
◆ Managing crises
◆ Maintaining entrepreneurial growth

as the rule rather than the exception. Interim management companies will, themselves, become either elephants or fleas over the next ten years or so.

What about the fleas? These are the small, entrepreneurial firms that will become more pronounced in the Information Age. They trade on the basis of brainpower, operating as software design, biotechnology, media, publishing, financial services and many other kinds of companies. They are fairly easy to set up because they require very little in the form of capital outlay. It is not the same as starting a small manufacturing business where premises and machinery are needed for trading purposes. All that is needed in an information-based business is the idea, a modem and a quiet room.

This is fine for a start-up, but it is not enough for a business that wants to grow. For this to happen, the business has to be promoted, cash flows have to be managed, new product lines explored, etc. All of these are skills that the founding entrepreneur may lack and may not be able to hire in on a permanent basis.

The years 1999 and 2000 witnessed the demise of many dot.com companies. Had these businesses benefited from more experienced management talent, many of their mistakes could have been avoided and investors' money saved. In other words, here was a great opportunity to capitalise on the talents of interim managers. Clearly, the experience of these dot.com companies demonstrates that the senior managers of corporate elephants do not have a monopoly on business arrogance. A further factor is swelling the importance of interim management – the changing psychology of managers themselves. Fewer of them want long-term careers in companies (even if these are available). Instead, they want to exercise their personal talents to the full. They are looking for continuous change, challenge and excitement in their work. They do not want to be accountable to line managers except on a short-term basis. They think of their lives as a series of projects, both in terms of home and work. Interim management offers them a model of work that is entirely compatible with this sea change in their ways of thinking. If companies want to capture the highest calibre talent, they will have no choice but to draw more heavily on the services of interim management companies than they may have done up to now.

Promoting creativity in the knowledge business

The twenty-first century will witness the continuing growth of the information economy, with businesses trading on the basis of various value-added services that they can provide. This means that their key asset is brain power and not, as in the past, machinery and the capacity to produce standardised products for either high volume or niche markets (as is the case for large numbers of small and medium-sized enterprises).

In order for companies to be competitive in the information economy, they need to redesign their operational processes, management styles and compliant cultures.

Intellectual capital refers to the knowledge that a company possesses in order to be innovative in continuously developing new products and services that are relevant for gaining competitive advantage in their targeted markets. In other words, in an information economy, brain power is the basis for a company's core competencies. Everything else that may have been undertaken within traditional, highly integrated enterprises can now be outsourced, often on a global basis. The key challenge for businesses at the start of the twenty-first century is to nurture creativity and innovation. It is the ability to do this that will differentiate successful, high-performing, and competitive businesses from the rest.

How can creativity be nurtured in businesses so that there is continuous innovation? In many ways, there are lessons to be learned from the ways in which many small and medium-sized enterprises operate. Those that are high performing have clarity of vision. The founding owners have a clear idea of where they want their businesses to go. But, an additional and vital ingredient is that so, too, do their employees. In other words, there is an employer-employee partnership in which the vision is shared. To implement this simple principle, however, requires the presence of a range of organisational features. First, that there is open, honest and fluid communication around all matters that are likely to affect the company's future. Second, this, in turn, demands the existence of a culture of high trust between employers and employees. Third, this, in itself, requires that employees are trained and given the capacity to develop their own talents for their own self-development as well as for the good of the enterprise. They must feel themselves as stakeholders, participating in the rewards of the company as it grows. This can be in a variety of forms ranging from equity stakes (as in many business partnerships) to profit sharing and career prospects.

It is in these organisational contexts that creativity is nurtured. These features account for the rapid growth of many small and medium-sized ventures in such diverse industries as high technology, bioscience, professional services, advertising and entertainment. Often such organisational attributes are structured around the 'charisma' or the personalities of the founder-owners. Although this can be an advantage, it is not a necessity. But what is vital for high performance is continuous innovation by promoting the creativity of employees through developing the appropriate organisational processes.

Product innovation through employee creativity requires a redefined psychological contract between employer and employee. It demands a shift from employee compliance to corporate commitment. Essentially, this means that employees are excited by their jobs – they eat, sleep and drink their work. Their jobs are at the heart of their personal identities. It is only through managing the business as a partnership between employers and employees that this can be achieved. This can often have ramifications for the design and location of businesses.

If, in the past, the workplace was the place where work was done, in the information economy it is the place where ideas are exchanged and problems solved. This normally requires close working relationships among colleagues and the cultivation of positive team dynamics. It not only places a premium on selecting potential employees who are technically competent but also on recruiting people who are personally compatible with each other. It also means that the architecture and the design of the workplace needs to encourage employee sociability.

What is striking about businesses that compete on the basis of their intellectual capital is how they convey the physical impression that nothing much is being produced. This is because the workplace is designed to encourage face-to-face encounters among colleagues for the purposes of problem solving and for the generation of new ideas. This means that a high proportion of floor space is designated as 'public areas', consisting of comfortable sofas arranged around vending machines. These areas are the nerve centres of creative businesses. Through discussion in these areas, colleagues develop ideas and then return to their 'private spheres' (and this is increasingly the home instead of the workplace) to explore further their potential and feasibility. These thoughts will then be fed back to colleagues in the coffee area on a later occasion.

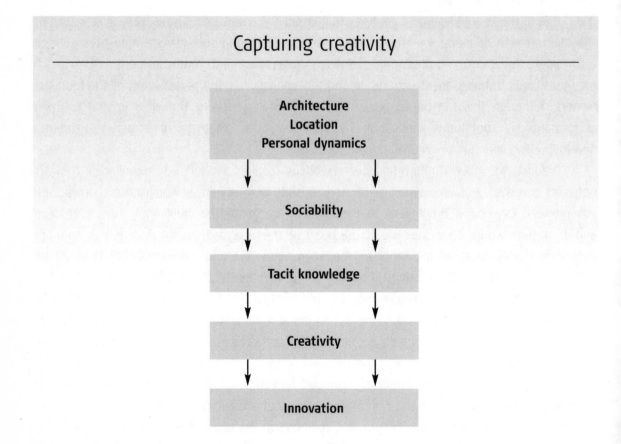

A significant feature of this is that the innovative process is not formally structured. It is not a specialist or compartmentalised activity, as is often the case in traditional manufacturing companies. Instead, it is located at the very heart of the business process and is essentially informal and unstructured. Employers cannot tell employees to be creative. Intellectual capital does not operate in this way. But what employers can do is to provide the organisational and architectural contexts that facilitate employee creativity and then reward employees so that they have a stakeholder interest in the innovative outcomes. This often means more than simply

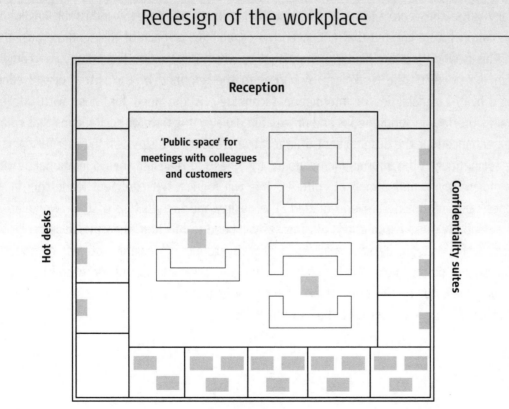

Redesign of the workplace

Reception

'Public space' for meetings with colleagues and customers

Hot desks

Confidentiality suites

Project rooms

material rewards. It can be part-ownership of patents, as in bioscience, or the opportunity for professional recognition, as in the entertainment industry.

Location is also an important factor for promoting creativity and fully utilising the intellectual capital of a business. Why is it that the centre of the global entertainment industry continues to be located in congested Los Angeles? Why do advertising agencies locate in parts of London and software companies in the Thames Valley? It is because these geographical areas constitute clusters of tacit knowledge, of intellectual skills from which all firms benefit. Pools of talent become geographically concentrated and then shape the character of local infrastructures. In this way, local labour markets from which companies recruit are reservoirs of intellectual capital. In many ways, these are similar to the industrial districts of the early Industrial Revolution. In these, cultures were created that enhanced the capabilities of each of the separate businesses.

This is why there are limits to the extent to which information technology can completely abolish the need for the workplace. A barrier to the adoption of the virtual organisation, as enabled by the capabilities of information technology, is the need for those with intellectual capital to interface in spontaneous and unstructured ways. It is through such means that creativity can be enhanced for the development of innovative products and services. In order for companies to be competitive in the information economy, they need to redesign their operational processes, management styles and compliant cultures. This will require self-confident leadership in which openness and informality are encouraged. The design and architecture of their workplaces will need to embody these assumptions. Businesses will need to function as partnerships in all of their aspects, from strategic decision-making to the structuring of reward systems. Without these mechanisms in place, intellectual capital – as the core asset of information-based businesses – will simply walk out of the door. Unlike machinery in factories, people – especially those with creative knowledge – cannot be bolted to the floor.

Creativity and forces for disorganisation

Customer knowledge is needed to guide R & D, marketing and sales functions. Customer-driven cultures have to be established that pervade all aspects of a business. Without this, there can be heavy investment in capital and human resources for manufacturing products and services for which there is no demand. This is why customer relationship management (CRM) is becoming a corporate priority. Collaborative relations with business partners in order to collect and share data is vital for the product development process. But this is not enough. Customer data, in itself, does not allow businesses to be innovative.

Managing employee creativity is often so challenging that many companies prefer to be 'average performing', by sticking to traditional management practices and structures.

As we all know too well, most of our businesses are flooded with too much data. We are overloaded with the customer information that modern technologies are able to provide us. Equally, customer data only provides partially adequate customer knowledge. The sophisticated technologies of retailers provide them with knowledge of customers' past purchasing patterns. It does not allow for detailed projections of how these are likely to change in the future. The checkout technologies of superstores may inform store managers of what customers have bought. But they do not disclose data on what customers have not bought. Surely this is more important for product development? To be useful for strategic purposes, customer data has to be interpreted, analysed and even 'played with'. It is this 'next-step' activity that is the basis for business modelling and future scenarios of customer behaviour. It is this that turns information-rich businesses into intelligent corporations. Customer *intelligence* rather than customer *knowledge* is the killer application.

Although software engineers design the most sophisticated tools for data management and analysis, they have – so far – failed to develop technologies that supercede the human brain. It is human creativity, in conjunction with information and communication technologies, that develops innovative products and services. The dominance of software cultures within businesses creates conformity, an excessive (and unrealistic) belief in the infallibility of technologies, and the under-valuation of employee abilities. The result is a rigidity in operating processes from which we often suffer when dealing with call centres. A challenge for leading-edge companies is for them to promote the creativity in their human cultures rather than placing inflated expectations on what information technologies can deliver.

Corporate culture-building programmes, more often than not, are exercises in reinforcing employee compliance and conformity. Staff are encouraged to think in terms of the 'corporate way of doing things' and to internalise dominant ways of doing things through their attitudes and behaviour. This is exactly the opposite of what businesses need if they are to be high performing and innovative. What companies should be doing is encouraging their employees to 'be different', individualistic, non-conformist and, most importantly of all, to challenge the taken-for-granted ways of doing things. Leaders and managers should be providing environments in which their staff feel comfortable to question the ways in which business is being conducted, and to come forward with new ideas and suggestions and to be critical of existing practices. A culture has to be sustained that distinguishes between 'positive' and 'negative' criticism.

To create these cultures often demands a change in recruitment practices. In too many businesses, the pattern is to select personnel who demonstrate the ability to 'fit in'. In other words, to conform and to comply with the status quo. CVs that indicate too many career changes are discarded on the basis they reflect personal 'instability'. A contrary interpretation could be that frequent job shifts reflect personal flexibility and the personal experience of a broad range of work environments. These can suggest that individuals are independent-minded, non-conformist, possibly difficult to work with and, maybe, highly critical of others. And it is this that is the problem for many companies. On the one hand, they want to have creative, innovative corporate cultures. But, on the other, they are reluctant to recruit those who have exactly the personal attributes to bring this about. This creates tensions in high-performing businesses. The 'split-personality' company, which tries to give employees working autonomy but within tight performance-related constraints, is a response to this. But there are further forces that are likely to undermine corporate commitment when there are attempts to build creative cultures.

One such force is that creative employees are inclined to be highly individualistic and unprepared to cooperate with others. They are likely to keep new ideas to themselves unless these can be used to further their own personal goals. Linked to this, they often regard their employers as resource pools that can be exploited for their own personal gain. This can be the case in media companies. Producers, writers, editors, etc, use their employers' resources for the pursuit of their personal careers. This is why they frequently move from one employer to the next. Only as long as they are given the budgets and the resources to achieve their 'creative' goals, will they stay with their present company. If these are bettered by a competitor company, they move on. Employing companies can only respond by offering more resources, higher material rewards and by appealing to their superior brand reputation. Many creative employees stick with their employers because of this. They will often do so even in the face of the offer of higher financial incentives from elsewhere.

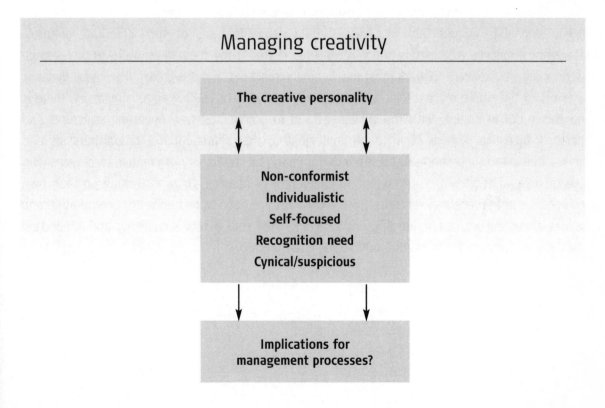

Managing creativity

The creative personality

Non-conformist
Individualistic
Self-focused
Recognition need
Cynical/suspicious

Implications for management processes?

If creative personnel are prepared to work in teams, it can be either because they can use the skills of colleagues for their own ends or because they enjoy working with others with similar personality attributes. But such groupings of employees can create counter cultures within businesses; cultures that breed cynicism and sometimes resentment. When this becomes pronounced, there is corporate fragmentation. The business breaks into clans, consisting of diverse groups of individuals who have allegiance to their colleagues and (sometimes) immediate bosses but with little or no commitment to their employing organisations. Only the corporate brand and the monthly salary cheque keep the business together. This is a feature of many advertising agencies, broadcasting companies, universities, hospitals and professional practices. But it is also found in software companies, R & D institutes and other knowledge-based businesses where intellectual capital is the operating core.

These are major challenges for businesses in the twenty-first century. They demand new organisational paradigms that recognise the distinctive features of such corporate cultures. Managing employee creativity is often so challenging that many companies prefer to be 'average performing', by sticking to traditional management practices and structures. The more dynamic markets of the future make it less likely these will survive. For leading edge companies, there is no choice but to grapple with the challenges and to accept that new operating structures and personal incentive systems have to be implemented, that share options, co-partnerships and stakes in intellectual property rights are vital for capturing the loyalty of creative employees who are capable, at short notice, of moving to competitor companies. Or even, setting up their own competitive entrepreneurial ventures. Such companies will need to recognise that corporate brand values are as important for selecting and retaining their core assets – creativity and intellectual capital – as they are for marketing and selling their products.

Valuing creativity and intellectual capital

The shift from economies based on manufacturing to those organised around knowledge and intellectual capital raises major problems for corporate treasurers. How do you value these businesses? What is their price in negotiations during mergers and acquisitions? How can these assets be valued and, just as importantly, measured in a quantifiable and consistent fashion? The same problems are associated with the corporate brand. Is this an appreciating or depreciating asset? Can there ever be objective criteria for corporate valuations or is it simply 'your guess is as good as mine'? It seems to be the latter.

It is only by understanding customers' wants and preferences that companies can develop innovative products and services.

This was convincingly illustrated by the dot.com bubble and burst when, within a matter of months, the valuation of these businesses plummeted by an average of ninety-five percent. At their height, the expectation was that their future earnings potential was huge. This was built on the assumption that customer knowledge and software technologies would destroy the old economy. They were valued on the basis of two key factors. The first, an assessment of their earnings potential. The second, on assumptions about the quality of their intangible assets for generating these future earnings. Their stock values in no way reflected balance sheet tangibles, such as buildings, equipment and technological hardware. When only a few of these businesses reported cash-flow problems and trading losses, the whole dot.com boom burst.

Whether in media agencies, management consultancies or even transnational pharmaceutical corporations, there is a growing reliance on intellectual capital assets. The value of corporate brands, that are derived from the continuous renovation and renewal of product and service portfolios, are ultimately driven by these. Destroy the quality of intellectual capital within a business and what is the value of a management consultancy, legal practice or a biotechnology company? Even so, the intellectual capital of a business can never precisely be measured. This is because the potential for generating corporate value can never be made fully explicit.

In this sense, modern corporations function as icebergs. The one-seventh that is visible is probably less important, as the *Titanic* found, than the six-sevenths that are concealed below the water. It is here that the intellectual assets and, hence, the value of the business, are hidden. This is often why so many high-performing corporations are willing to have case studies written about them and to be subject to detailed study by outsiders. They know very well that the practices that make them so successful cannot be imitated. They evolve a 'way of doing things', a methodology that is understood by all those working in the business so that no explicit criteria for operations have to be formulated. But, alongside the importance of this tacit knowledge is the fact that much of the value of a company's intellectual capital is tied into external business relationships. This consists of two key elements. The first is customer relations. The second is partnerships with other supply-chain businesses; manufacturers, suppliers and retailers.

The quality of intellectual capital is heavily dependent upon customer intelligence. It is only by understanding customers' wants and preferences that companies can develop innovative products and services. But, in more dynamic markets where consumers are more cynical and less loyal to product and corporate brands, the knowledge of the customer today may not help to develop product strategies for the future. In recent years, much attention has been given to the need for companies to develop their core competencies. This has often led to an excessive focus on the marketplace of today with the disregard of trends that are likely to affect consumer markets of the future. That is why so many major retailers experience fluctuating fortunes. Their 'close to the customer' strategies become counter-productive and, often, implosive. Hence, it becomes difficult to value the intellectual capital of a business since its core competencies of today may mitigate against competitive advantage in the future. Attempts by management consultancies to factor this in by constructing 'indices of innovation' and 'rates of new products to market' can only partly capture this aspect of a company's intellectual capital assets.

The same problem applies to business partnerships, joint ventures and strategic alliances. Often, these allow companies to concentrate upon specialist trading activities because of their compatible, collaborative relations. Through these, the value of intellectual capital within each of the separate businesses can be enhanced. Synergies and cost reductions may be gained through the pooling of human and technical resources. But the point is that, remove a business from a strategic alliance or joint venture and the value of its own 'standalone' intellectual capital is reduced as a competitive asset.

Those with the skills that make up the core competencies of a business can walk out of the door in very unpredictable and temperamental ways. This can be triggered by a change in corporate leadership, management style or even by rumours of redundancy and company downsizing. There are also the continuing appeals of offers from competing employers, to say nothing of the fact that barriers to business start-up for many of those who work with their brains is often very low. Creatives in advertising agencies, film producers, actuaries, fund managers and even scientists and technologists can engage in entrepreneurial ventures more easily than those with skills in traditional manufacturing. The start-up costs are often lower and, even when high capital funding may be needed, those with high personal brand reputations can have little difficulty in attracting the attention of venture capitalists.

The mobility of intellectual assets is often an issue in mergers and acquisitions. If, as the result of being merged or acquired, those with the brains quit the business, what is to be gained? Maybe the purchase of a well-recognised, highly regarded corporate brand. But how long is this likely to last if those with the intellectual skills leave the business? It is rather pointless buying a highly rated restaurant if the chef decides to quit. But intellectual capital can also become redundant. Without investment in continuous professional and technical training, skills can

Managing intellectual capital

Problems of valuing:

- Intangible assets
- Tacit knowledge
- Business partner 'lock-ins'
- Customer knowledge
- Corporate brand values
- Future net earnings

become obsolete. This applies to scientists and technologists as well as to designers, architects, scriptwriters, programme producers and musicians. With ageing and the lack of appropriate incentives, they can lose interest, become disenchanted and de-motivated. Those with intellectual capital do not go on strike. They have no need to. They can cease to come forward with new ideas for R & D, develop 'writer's block' and produce (what they know to be) poor advertising campaigns. They can behave in exactly the same way as disenchanted musicians, baseball and soccer players. They may be under contract to their employers but, if they choose to under-perform, there is little the other party can do. Mysteriously, demotivated baseball and soccer players have a greater frequency of injuries while dissatisfied singers develop throat infections.

Retaining corporate intellectual capital assets is leading to the introduction of new reward systems and employment relations. It is forcing companies to develop socially responsible brand reputations and to introduce share-options and co-ownership of intellectual property rights, as in the pharmaceutical industries. The greater mobility of those with creative and intellectual assets is adding to corporate uncertainties. This adds greater complexity to the valuation of businesses in an ever-changing corporate world of mergers and acquisitions. These are, in turn, reinforced by the difficulties of valuing these assets. Perhaps companies should follow the example of UK soccer clubs. Their celebrity players, purchased for millions of pounds, are regarded as being of nil value in company assets.

The importance of the corporate event and sociability

For many companies, corporate events are vitally important. Although the formal agenda may be to approve strategic plans, their real contribution is to bring together colleagues who would otherwise never see each other. This is particularly important for global corporations. Their project teams may be organised to interact through Internet technologies but for trust and the exchange of ideas to develop, periodic face-to-face contact is vital. All such approaches to encouraging face-to-face interaction attempt to nurture tacit knowledge – to encourage colleagues to understand how others work. This

Office chat is the basis for new ideas and out of these come innovation and competitive advantage.

strengthens our own personal competencies but, at the same time, makes us interdependent. Because we work well together, we become good at one thing because our colleagues are good at something else. I can concentrate on developing my particular strengths and so can you. In this way, we complement each other. We even become dependent upon each other in the exercise of our own personal skills. We understand how each other thinks and how we each prefer to do different things in an informal but clearly understood division of labour. Only face-to-face sociability allows this to happen. The real key to high performance is through combining individual talents through shared understanding and 'hidden' knowledge gained through intensive organisational sociability. Many small firms are good at this, particularly if they are located in geographical clusters that facilitate after-hours contacts.

For large corporations, however, sociability has to be encouraged through organising major employee events. Indeed the spend on in-house corporate events seems to be holding up. Even in times of economic downturn, companies are reluctant to cut their budgets for off-site meetings that are becoming ever grander. Locations are becoming more exotic and facilities ever more luxurious. The larger corporations put up gigantic stage sets, complete with speaker auto-cues, laser lighting and stereo surround sound. Then there are the gurus, the entertainment and the celebrity after-dinner speakers. At a recent corporate event in Europe, the U.S. keynote speaker charged $100,000 plus airfares and all expenses. For this, he chatted off the cuff for forty minutes, tossing out his thoughts on how he saw the future of the Internet.

What do delegates gain? Quite a lot. A range of factors is driving the growing popularity of such events. We now work in corporate structures that are highly fragmented. Project management is the order of the day. We identify with these rather than the broader company picture. The company event brings us together in celebration of corporate mission, vision and culture. It is rather like going to church, reaffirming our beliefs and corporate identities. The occasion has to offer something special though. As employees, we have access to exclusive knowledge or information not available to others. This is where the gurus kick in. They are sharing their wisdom with us. Then the message has to be put across that this is a 'fun' company to work for. Not only is the event about forward planning and debating corporate strategy but also about having a good time. That is why celebrity speakers are rolled out.

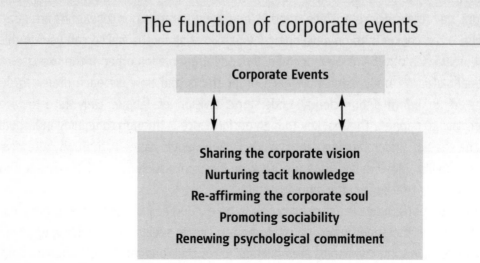

The function of corporate events

Corporate Events

Sharing the corporate vision
Nurturing tacit knowledge
Re-affirming the corporate soul
Promoting sociability
Renewing psychological commitment

There is also the message that this is an exciting company to work for. That is why there are often such events as go-kart racing and water sports, intensifying emotional and psychological bonds between employer and employee. Through these events, the company develops an identity. By linking ourselves with this, employees become more motivated and, even, inspired. When competitive advantage is based on high rates of product and service innovation, it means that a high premium is attached to promoting employee brainpower. To do this, staff must feel good about their companies. If the corporate event succeeds, perhaps it is not a waste of money after all.

But is this just a load of talk? In the high-performing company, generating a high level of sociability among colleagues becomes a key strategic issue. As we now spend much of our time staring at computer screens, we have to be encouraged to talk to each other. Why is this important? Because office chat is the basis for new ideas and out of these come innovation and competitive advantage. Research on high-performing high-tech companies confirms this. What separates these companies from the rest is the intensity of personal networks and contacts among colleagues. Premises are planned to encourage face-to-face communication. Coffee machines are installed in the middle of work areas so that people bump into each other. Chief executives locate their offices so that colleagues can drop in on an informal and frequent basis. But, most importantly, a high premium is attached to out-of-hours socialisation. Why do many companies stay in large towns with their high costs, congestion and overcrowded facilities. Instead of relocating to the more congenial rural environments? Because of the absence of a high geographical concentration of pubs, restaurants and wine bars. It is in these places that colleagues meet up and it is here that the corporate plans are prepared, innovative ideas developed and sales leads pursued. In small businesses, there is no need for the corporate event because working for the company is a corporate event every day. To move from these facilities would, quite literally, destroy not only the heart and soul of these businesses but also the core of their strategic and operational processes. What is also interesting is that their costs are kept low and their productivity high because out-of-hours sociability reduces the need for meetings during 'normal' working time. This practice also generates commitment and, among colleagues, a clear understanding of the company's strategy into which they all make an impact.

These companies are also very open in sharing their strategies with their customers and other business partners. This culture encourages strategic alliances and joint ventures for product development. There is an absence of corporate paranoia and obsession with secrecy. Why? Because these businesses know that their practices cannot be imitated. Based as they are on tacit working relations and built upon intense personal relations, they know their ideas cannot be stolen. Why are celebrity chefs in demand even though they sell their recipes as books? Because, although they put their ideas into the public domain, they know that their special and very personal set of cooking techniques cannot be imitated. And so it is with large high-performing companies. Sociability and tacit knowledge have to be nurtured through the corporate event.

Section 4

On the work-life tight rope

Balancing home and work

In today's world, work-life balance is a major political issue. It is on the agenda of governments in the United Kingdom, France, Germany and Scandinavia. In the United States, as in Europe, corporations are addressing what has become a key employee priority – how to balance the demands of work and career with those of personal relations and psychological well being.

When we are struggling with a particular work problem, can we ever truly switch off and psychologically disengage ourselves even when we are at home?

In the past, these matters were less pronounced. The old bureaucracies and regimented labour markets reinforced a sharp distinction between home and work. So, too, did traditional gender roles and lifestyles. Each of these forces has been demolished, creating ambiguities and uncertainties as to how we structure our lives and the positioning of work within them.

In the old days, we worked from nine to five or thereabouts. Occasionally, there would be pressing matters that would force us to take work home. But generally work processes were organised so that they should be undertaken according to strict operating procedures. Personal performance was measured in terms of compliance to procedures. This was the priority for office managers and corporate bosses. The needs of customers were normally considered as secondary and it was regarded as simply 'too bad' if things were running behind, meetings postponed and goods delivered late. The length of the working day defined what was and what was not done.

This pattern was reinforced by the role of strong trade unions first in manufacturing and then in the expanding administrative and service sectors of national economies. As a part of negotiating over job descriptions and payment systems, length of working hours was central. Agreements over 'normal working hours' allowed employees to enhance their earnings through working overtime for which additional rates of pay would be offered to compensate for what were usually considered asocial hours.

The sharp distinction between home and work was also upheld by traditional gender roles. For married couples, men went out to work and women stayed at home. Men could pursue their careers with the guaranteed certainty that they had female partners for life and that these would service their personal and lifestyle needs. It meant that men could be focused on their jobs since the domestic sphere could be delegated to women. The home was a refuge from work and the basis for a leisure identity. Female partners were often symbols of consumption and reflected the career success of their male partners. Rarely did work activities, either functionally or psychologically, invade the private and personal, home-based sphere. This was infringed by employees' corporations on only two very infrequent occasions. One of which was when there was the occasional need to take work home, usually to read a report in preparation for a next-day meeting. The other was when colleagues were invited home for dinner. Such an event constituted a strictly structured ritual that allowed the employee to demonstrate his respectability, domestic stability and, hence, suitability for further career enhancement.

The work-life distinction was further separated by travel and transport patterns. Employees travelled to and from work. As they do today. But there was little travel to business meetings with clients and customers. Communication was through postal correspondence and over the telephone. There was very limited travel overseas in the days of pre-globalisation. The outcome was that work patterns were predictable and that office and home-based activities could be kept separate from each other.

Today, working and personal lives could not be more different. The traditional distinction between home and work has evaporated. So, too, the notion of clearly defined and strictly adhered-to working hours. A key driver is the introduction of project-management principles. Work tasks are organised on the basis of customer-driven projects. Projects are costed and resourced according to budgets. These, by definition, incorporate uncertainties that can never be fully predicted. Unforeseen problems arise that lead to cost overshoots and under-resourcing. Staff fall ill, problems have to be solved, but the projects have to be completed on time. The outcome is working long hours, late in the evenings and at weekends. It means, over time, that leisure patterns and personal lifestyles can never be planned ahead. The consequence is that we work for what may be regarded as 'greedy' corporations. Employers that always have first call on our services and to which personal lifestyles must be subordinated.

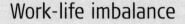

Work-life imbalance

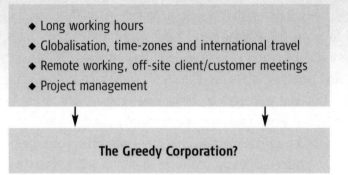

- Long working hours
- Globalisation, time-zones and international travel
- Remote working, off-site client/customer meetings
- Project management

The Greedy Corporation?

The decline of trade unionism and globalisation has made this issue more acute. No longer can the demands of the 'greedy' corporation be resisted through collective bargaining. We personally negotiate our psychological contracts with our employers. Those who are unprepared to work at weekends to complete projects – notwithstanding corporate value statements about employee quality of life – are seen to be uncommitted and to lack dedication to the corporation. Peer-group pressure from colleagues leads to ostracism and social isolation if anyone chooses to give priority to their personal lives over getting projects completed in time. To do so, in a genuine sense, is to let down colleagues in their endeavour to achieve their goals and to receive performance-related rewards.

The globalisation of business transactions that has exploded with the liberalisation of international trade and through mega-corporate mergers and acquisitions, has destroyed predictable work patterns. The operation of time zones has created 24/7 corporate realities; twenty-four hours a day, seven days a week. The functioning of multinational business on this basis has knock-on effects for all other economic sectors. The travel and transport industries, petrol stations, fast-food outlets, supermarkets are all, in their different ways, affected by the variable working hours and flexible demands of those directly affected by globalisation. These trends can only increase as the impact of the global economy becomes even more pronounced over the next decades.

One such impact is the demand for international travel. The Internet age creates greater needs for face-to-face meetings and personal negotiations. The telecommunications revolution facilitates rather than displaces demands for business travel. So, too, does a culture of customer relationship management. To demonstrate our commitment to our customers, we meet them face-to-face, entertain them and organise major corporate events for them. It means that sales and marketing executives are constantly on the move, travelling within regions and across time zones. The resultant knock-on effects are the demands they place on their office-based colleagues to be on-call 24/7 to follow up customer enquiries and expectations.

In a business environment when, potentially, corporations set no limits on the demands they have on their employees, how are our work-life boundaries to be established? What constitutes a healthy and satisfactory work-life balance? When are corporations placing excessive demands on their employees? When does the pursuit of an acceptable work-life balance spill over to lack of corporate commitment and letting the team down? These are just some of the fundamental questions that are being asked among a growing number of corporations and their employees. In the old days of industrial manufacturing, the answers were given to us in written rules and procedures. Today, the global-based information economy asks new questions, arising from the ambiguities and uncertainties surrounding project-driven work processes, customer-focused business solutions and the need to exercise personal intellectual skills. In fact, when we are struggling with a particular work problem, can we ever truly switch off and psychologically disengage ourselves even when we are at home? But it is ourselves who will ultimately bear the cost. Other than some token corporate representatives, our funerals will be attended by family and friends. Did we ever have time to get to know them?

Dedicated to the corporation: who does it and for what?

Corporate commitment is the buzzword of the twenty-first century. It is no longer sufficient for us to be motivated in our jobs; we have to be committed to the corporation. Doctors are committed to their patients, teachers to their pupils and sales professionals to their customers.

It is among dual career couples that pressures surrounding the work-life balance are most pronounced, particularly among those with children.

But, again, this is not enough. It is also imperative to be committed to our employing organisations. That is, to be signed up to the mission statement, the value statement, the culture and the everyday pattern of rituals and personal expectations. But how do we demonstrate corporate commitment? How do employees operationally and personally articulate these in their working lives? This is the challenge and it is the pursuit of this that can destroy a satisfactory work-life balance.

Essentially, the personal demonstration of corporate commitment is to subscribe to the attributes and values of our line managers. That is, to project and team leaders and other operational heads. It entails the adherence to compliant dress codes, sharing common sports interests and having a compatible sense of humour. It generates interpersonal bonding upon which management trust and confidentiality are established. At the same time, of course, in view of the gender composition of senior corporate teams, it leads to feelings of marginality and corporate exclusion among female colleagues.

This same demonstration of corporate commitment can also lead to longer term company stagnation. Among colleagues, it can foster 'strong' corporate cultures of conformity and complacency. Management teams become composed of corporate lemmings. That is, of those who dare not challenge their line managers, ask awkward questions or even suggest new ideas for fear that these will disturb the status quo. Those who are sufficiently self-confident to do so – normally new recruits who have yet to understand fully the rules of the game and the tacit political processes – are seen to lack future management potential. They are seen to be uncooperative, poor team members and, at worst, uncommitted to the corporation. The demonstration of commitment, in other words, means accepting the established and taken-for-granted way of doing things. The outcome in many companies is a rhetoric of innovation and change, concealing a reality of conservatism and compliance.

The most important way to demonstrate corporate commitment is through personal visibility. This is the major factor accounting for the long-working-hours cultures of the United States and Britain. It is a further outcome of the structuring of companies on the basis of project-management teams and decentralised operating units. Even in the Internet age, when many of our tasks could be conducted at home, employees demonstrate their commitment by being first in the office in the morning and last out at night. Getting the project completed on time and within budget become prime factors in personal appraisal. The best way to achieve this is to work long hours.

Just as corporations have changed though, so too have their employees. No longer is there an almost total absence of women in management teams (although this varies from

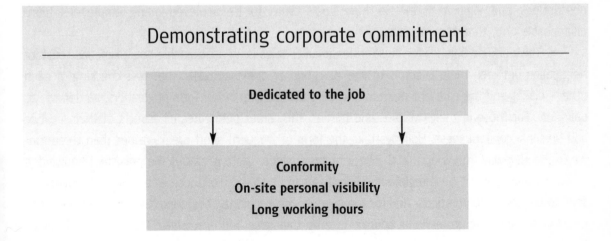

company to company and between economic sectors). Women make up a growing proportion of middle managers; a process which, in itself, is changing corporate culture and assumptions of personal trust and bonding relationships. Their further career advancement, however, is often jeopardised by male senior managers' prejudiced assumptions about the quality and intensity of their corporate commitment. More often than not, these assumptions are derived from expectations that women will behave as they have in the past. That is, that they live with male partners whose careers take precedence. Consequently, the argument is that female colleagues cannot be promoted to senior corporate positions. This is due to the risk that they will quit their jobs as a result of the need to be geographically mobile for their partners' jobs.

It is among dual career couples that pressures surrounding the work-life balance are most pronounced, particularly among those with children. Project management and performance related rewards can be incompatible with maternity, as well as paternity, leave. The assessment of company and, therefore, individual performance on a short-term quarterly basis cannot take full account of the corporate disturbances generated by such leaves of absence. In knowledge-based businesses, their dependence upon employees' skills, particularly their tacit understanding of how things are to be done, makes it more difficult to provide cover for leave of absence. Individuals are more indispensable than they were in the traditional bureaucracies. Then, clearly defined job descriptions and explicit details of how goals were to be achieved made employees more dispensable and, therefore, substitutable.

The work-life balance for most professional couples is an unattainable goal. It means constant negotiation between them in terms of the allocation of domestic tasks, the cross-checking of each other's diaries and the constant need to 'buy in' domestic help in the form of cleaners, gardeners, au pairs, etc. For those in their twenties and thirties, the career permeates all aspects of their lifestyle and personal consciousness. Holidays take the form of frequent short breaks rather than three/four week periods away from work. At the back of their minds, there is always the persistent knowledge that work tasks have to be completed and problems to be solved. For these employees, employers are seen to be greedy corporations. And for the overwhelming majority, this is exactly how they want it to be. How many young professional couples give up their jobs and downshift? The few who do make headline stories in the weekend newspaper supplements. But the most telling illustration of their love

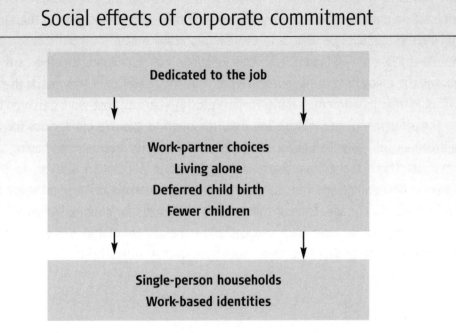

Social effects of corporate commitment

Dedicated to the job

Work-partner choices
Living alone
Deferred child birth
Fewer children

Single-person households
Work-based identities

for their jobs, their work teams and their employing corporations is the depression many women encounter when they give up their careers to have children. Focusing upon 'life' in the 'work-life' balance does not seem to compensate for the loss of the razzmatazz of the corporate world.

There is a further way of resolving the challenges of balancing work and leisure interests. If being with a partner creates contradictions only to be compounded by having children then avoid the problems in the first place. And this is what a rapidly growing number of men and women in the United States and Europe are choosing to do. They are the corporation men and women of the twenty-first century. They accept the priority demands of their work roles and their employing corporations. They therefore decide to stay single and to live alone. The magnitude of this trend in Europe is such that the population of many counties is in decline. Birth rates are falling as women in Scandinavia, the United Kingdom, France, Spain and Italy are deferring the age at which they have children. And when they do, they have far fewer children than in the past.

They are choosing to live alone since it allows them to avoid the complications of the work-life balancing act. In uncluttered ways, they can develop their talents and skills in their jobs, complete their projects (hopefully) on time and be geographically mobile in more extensive employment markets. For these men and women, partner relations will come later, together with the children. So, too, will the enjoyment of life outside work. This they defer until they reach their fifties when they will quit their jobs to enjoy thirty (or even forty) years of post-work personal creativity.

The affluence of the Information Age, the need to exercise intellectual skills at work and the difficulties of establishing a harmonious work-life balance is having fundamental repercussions. These range from macro-demographics in population decline, to the growth of single-person households and the early exit from labour markets of large numbers of employees when they reach middle age. Each of these poses challenges for national governments since they have ramifications for housing, care services and general age-related lifestyle facilities. Living in the corporate zoo can be fun but, some would say, comes with a price.

Working long hours

Work long hours or get a life? It seems a simple choice. The reality of the corporate zoo is there is no choice at all. The demonstration of commitment to the employing organisation demands long work hours. It is the visibility principle. But, at the same time, employees want to work long hours. Particularly those who have made the lifestyle choices – to put work and career before leisure and personal relations. For these employees, work is leisure and leisure is work. Work relations are personal relations and vice versa.

For these employees, aged in their twenties through to their early forties, it is their work and their corporate positions that give them their personal identities.

For these employees, aged in their twenties through to their early forties, it is their work and their corporate positions that give them their personal identities. It shapes their consciousness and their sense of being. In the pursuit of their performance targets, in being assessed according to corporate-defined key success factors, they shape their own particular wants and expectations. Their collaboration with colleagues in teams requires the exercise of interpersonal attitudes and behaviour that cannot be abandoned on leaving the workplace at the (late) end of the day. In the old bureaucracies, employees role-played, undertaking their tasks as cogs in corporate machines. The jobs of knowledge workers are far more demanding. The exercise of intellectual, social and emotional skills demands a heavy psychological input. The continuous need to keep up with new ideas, to solve problems and to deliver solutions, requires total emotional and psychological engagement. It demands the use of the whole personality rather than the exercise of purely technical skills acquired during corporate training programmes.

This is why knowledge workers love their jobs. By definition they have to, otherwise they would quit or be fired. The exercise of personal creativity and initiative is destroyed once employees lose interest in their work. As soon as their commitment wanes so, too, does the quality of their intellectual capital. But the high performers want to work and they do. Witness the long working hours of software designers, pharmaceutical researchers, advertising executives, medics and teachers. For each of these and many others, their jobs shape their personal identities.

However, it goes further than this. It is not only their occupations and jobs that motivate these people but also their corporate identities. This is why corporate brands are not only important for marketing strategies, but they are equally crucial for attracting and retaining high quality intellectual talent. Brand values in relation to sustainability, social responsibility, corporate governance and equal opportunities are the recruiter qualities that young job applicants consider when submitting their CVs. If they are to develop their personal identities on the basis of their corporate affiliations, there must be harmony in personal and corporate values. If personal reputation amongst peers in the community, as well as in labour markets, is determined by the brand of corporate employers, this is highly significant in developing personal career portfolios. It is particularly significant if the overwhelming percentage of waking hours is devoted, directly or indirectly, to work-related matters.

There is, however, a price to be paid. The commitment and the long working hours of employees are affecting family patterns and the nature of out-of-work personal relations. But it goes even further than this. It extends beyond the growth of single-person households and declining populations. It is affecting national social structures and patterns of economic and social inequalities. The long-working-hours culture of the United Kingdom and the United States is creating poverty, low wages and, with these, social exclusion. It is generating an underclass of employees who work in low-skill, low-paid and insecure jobs. In the absence of government regulation and intervention, it is leading to the emergence of a category of employees who are vulnerable and dependent upon the affluence and spending power of cash-rich, time-poor knowledge workers.

Owing to their long working hours, knowledge employees – as corporate men and women – do not have time to look after their children, to clean clothes or houses, to prepare evening meals and to tend to their gardens. The result is that they purchase the labour of others to provide these services which, if they had more time, they would do themselves. The outcome is a growing underclass of men and women who provide these services. It consists of students

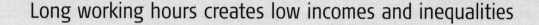

Long working hours creates low incomes and inequalities

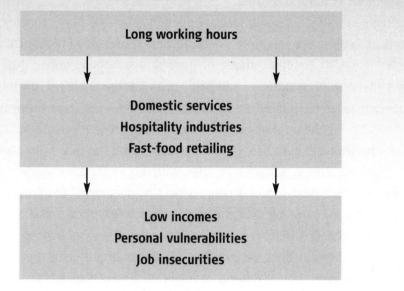

Long working hours

Domestic services
Hospitality industries
Fast-food retailing

Low incomes
Personal vulnerabilities
Job insecurities

working through college, single-parent women working flexibly because of their own domestic obligations, older men who have been made redundant through corporate rationalisation and, of course, immigrants, both legal and illegal. How, other than through the use of Mexican workers, would professional households in California cope with their day-to-day service needs?

The link between long working hours and the creation of a low-paid underclass can be understood by comparing the United States and the United Kingdom with the Scandinavian countries. In these, there is legislation that limits the length of weekly working hours. This is based upon a tradition of government intervention in the private sector where partnership arrangements have generated high-performing, innovative, steady growth economies. But in these countries, inequalities have failed to increase to the same extent as in the United States and the United Kingdom. In Sweden, gardeners, nannies, au pairs, cleaners and temporary immigrant domestic assistants are unknown. This is because with their shorter working hours, dual career couples undertake household tasks themselves. This leads to the absence of a socially excluded underclass in these countries.

The ramifications of growing inequalities generates not only economic polarisation but, also, resentment, protest and low trust. These become expressed in higher crime rates and other law and order issues. It creates cultures of poverty and, among young people in low-income families, expectations of dead-end, low-paid jobs. Intergenerational poverty cycles become established which government intervention finds difficult if not, in some circumstances, impossible to break. So, can legislation to restrict working hours be effective? It appears so in the Scandinavian countries and in France. But it is unlikely to be the case in the United States and in the United Kingdom. This is because of their different models of management. The Anglo-American organisational model, based upon project management, performance-related rewards and short-term business planning mitigates this. Rather different organisational models prevail in Scandinavia and France. But there is a further difference. The long-working-hours culture of the United States and Britain defines assumptions about employee commitment. A self-sustaining momentum is now in place that is difficult to eradicate. The capabilities of mobile telephone and Internet technologies may allow for remote working practices but these are impotent in the face of well-entrenched management cultures.

The relative weakness of labour unionism is also a factor that presents effective legal enforcement. So, too, the growth of self-employed consultants, freelance providers of various technical and expert services and flourishing small business sectors. All of these define features of the United States and United Kingdom economies that are different to those found in Scandinavia. But perhaps the major reason why legislation regulating length of working hours is likely to be ineffective is that corporate men and women in Britain and the United States love their jobs. They want to work. It defines their species being. Long working hours may destroy their health and encourage them to avoid making long-term commitments in their personal lives but that is the way they want it. They voluntarily choose to be encaged in the corporate zoo. At least until they reach their early to mid-forties when they start to consider their escape.

Joining the zoo: employees of the future

Changing demographics will affect employee profiles in the future. Managing cultural diversity will be a commonplace activity for corporate team leaders. Globalisation is leading to an increasing focus upon managing personnel across national borders, world regions and time zones. The greater mobility of young employees and their knowledge of alternative opportunities in different parts of the world is changing the staffing composition of large global corporations. Migratory patterns among those with high-demand personal talents and skills are diversifying the ethnic and national composition of corporate labour markets.

Workplace interpersonal relations and team dynamics are reinforced by out-of-work patterns of colleague sociability.

In the United States, there is a growing number of Spanish-speaking young people. These are predominantly located on the eastern and western seaboards of the country. Spanish is becoming as dominant as English in California. How will U.S. managers cope with this trend? Should they adapt their working practices and language codes? Or should they relocate to other parts of the United States or to India and other English-speaking regions of the world? This is a challenge that the high-technology and software companies of California and the Boston region will soon have to tackle.

In Europe, there is a growing shortage of young people. In the United Kingdom, those entering the labour market (aged between 16 and 24) declined by thirty percent over the 1990s. The trend will continue in the future as women, choosing to live alone and deferring childbirth, put work and career before having children. Even in Italy, France and Spain, with their more extended family forms and more family focused lifestyles, there are similar patterns.

Skills shortages are emerging that the future European economy will have to address. There are a number of strategies available to corporate leaders and national policy makers. For companies, they can shift their businesses elsewhere. Already, financial institutions in the United Kingdom are migrating many of their back-office data-processing and call-centre activities to India, Australia and other countries in the Far East. Some UK-based companies are beginning to relocate some of their back-office functions to take advantage of the under-utilised skills of the growing cadres of graduates in China for data-processing purposes. For Germany, the countries of central Europe and Russia offer similar opportunities. The Novosibirsk region of Russia has a large concentration of talented employees who were engaged in the state-owned research institutes and defence industries of the old Soviet bloc. German companies are seizing upon these skills to train software engineers, designers and other computer-related employees.

The alternative to exporting jobs is to import skills. From this is emerging a twin-track immigration system in the United States and Europe. One track is directed towards the sifting and sorting of those with low-skill capabilities who are destined to work in the low-wage personal-service sector. These applicants are compelled by national governments to be processed through cumbersome bureaucratic processes before their applications for work are approved. They are a feature of a growing U.S. and European underclass, supplemented by others who by-pass these procedures by being 'illegal' immigrants.

The other track is the 'fast route' that national governments are increasingly using to meet national skills shortages. For these people, the experiences could not be more different. They are offered incentives, ranging from the payment of accommodation costs through to free travel and job-related training. The United Kingdom government, for example, is meeting nursing shortages in the state health service by recruiting in the Philippines and teacher shortages by attracting those with the required skills in Australia and Canada.

The outcome of each of these trends is the emergence of highly diverse national labour markets, interconnected through the impact of globalisation. The result is the emergence of corporate employee profiles, management teams and business units that consist of personnel with diverse backgrounds, experiences and expectations. Meeting and harmonising these for promoting corporate performance becomes a challenge for a growing number of line managers in the modern corporation. Differing work expectations among diverse employees can affect the ways they respond to authority, cooperate with others in teams, share ideas and the rewards that they hope to receive.

All of these trends, however, are occurring within broader cultural change that is affecting the operating processes and management practices of large companies. This is a cultural change that is being driven by the aspirations of young people in Europe and the United States. They have seen the unfulfilled expectations of their parents (mainly fathers) in their own career pursuits. They have witnessed how companies can swiftly dispense with personnel who have devoted their working lives to the good of their employing corporations. The children of these parents want none of it.

Instead of the promise of careers, young people have different demands of their employing organisations. With a predominantly instrumental approach to the employment relationship – I will give to them in return for what they will give to me – they expect to be offered opportunities for personal development and skill enhancement before they move on to the next corporate employment opportunity. Essentially, they are searching for challenges. But, even more than that, they are seeking excitement in their jobs. Their psychological focus is predominantly on the 'now' and the 'present' rather than on the 'future'. It is short-term rather than long-term. It is hedonistic instead of deferred gratification. In other words, no longer can corporate and team leaders recruit and attract talented young people on the promise of rewards in the future. The nature of their jobs has to be such that the psychological and material rewards are available to them today. Financial institutions played a key role in changing these employment expectations during the late 1980s. They established a role model that has now become widely disseminated within all sectors of the labour market.

All companies and organisations are being forced to respond to this quest for excitement and immediate material reward. The appeal to altruism and contributing to the common good of society is no longer enough to attract teachers, social workers, medics and others engaged in national public sectors. Government employees now have to compete for talent offering incentives and rewards in competition with those private-sector companies that offer personal challenge and excitement.

Exciting jobs are those that are emotionally and psychologically enjoyable. They are the occupations that give employees a 'buzz' and a good-time feel. Some companies are able to do this and while others are not. Entrepreneurial businesses are often able to strengthen the talents and contributions of their staff through making their jobs exciting. This encourages the full flow

of ideas, creativity and innovation. Those who find these jobs 'boring' quickly exit from these businesses because they are no longer able to fit in.

The dot.com companies offered a new model of organisation. One that was structured around youth, individuality, personal creativity, risk and uncertainty. New dress codes became adopted, unconventional forms of decision-making were set up and they turned upside down conventional business practices. The reason for this was that these young entrepreneurs understood the rewards and incentives that excite young people in general. All of this is in sharp contrast to the predominant compliant cultures and management practices of traditional large manufacturing enterprises. A key legacy of the dot.com boom is that it made transparent how young people prefer to work and what it is that stimulates and them.

There are, however, further implications. Young employees attach priority to quality of life as this is structured around their work experiences. Work is their central life interest and it shapes their identities and lifestyles. It means that work location becomes a key factor. For them, the world's major cities are becoming more attractive as places to live. This is reflected in the ratio of house prices to personal earnings. It is in these cities that young people can extend their experiences of excitement and fun from the workplace into leisure. The two collapse into one. Wine bars, coffee shops, restaurants and clubs become locations where work issues are discussed with colleagues, where problems are solved and creative ideas worked through. Workplace interpersonal relations and team dynamics are reinforced by out-of-work patterns of colleague sociability.

This means that in recruiting talented knowledge employees it is not only corporate brand and reward systems that are important. It is also insufficient to offer creativity, challenge and excitement in the workplace. Location also becomes a prime consideration. If work drives lifestyle and lifestyle shapes performance at work, where the company is located becomes key. This is why so many companies refuse to move from congested city environments to out-of-town green-field sites. The absence of entertainment and leisure facilities would destroy colleague sociability and, with it, corporate creativity and innovation. In a global economy, regional clusters of like-minded business activities, even in an Internet age, restrict the location of the corporate zoo.

Release from the cage:
the lure of early retirement

It is well known that Europe is ageing. It will experience an increase in life expectancy over the next decade, creating an older, dependent population. This will have a huge direct, as well as indirect, impact on the economy. It is a demographic time bomb that will affect both labour and consumer markets. As part of this trend, the fifty-something age group is expanding. Baby boomers have reached maturity. From twenty percent of the population today, they will grow to make up twenty-five percent over the next few years. Yet fewer of them are in full-time employment. In Britain, the proportion of fifty-five year-old men in employment has fallen from ninety-three percent in the 1970s to seventy-five percent today, while, for women, it has remained constant at about sixty percent. Consider that this is happening when skills shortages are growing. The number of young people entering the labour markets is declining sharply as a result of falling birth rates in the 1970s and 1980s. A key issue is whether Europe, and the United Kingdom in particular, can continue to accept such a low labour-market participation rate among fifty-year-olds. On the face of it, it suggests a great under-utilisation of talent and skills.

Making employment more enjoyable and less stressful would reduce the attractions of early retirement for professionals, managers and others whose skills are in demand.

Are those in their fifties being pushed out of their jobs or pulled by the attractions of life after work? The answer seems to be both. Corporate restructuring continues to be a major factor. The application of information and communication technologies has allowed companies to automate their management processes. This does not mean the end of hierarchical controls. On the contrary, information technology allows for even stricter monitoring of performance – even if we work from home. But it does not require layers of managers. Middle managers in their fifties are usually the first to be earmarked to go. It is the same with corporate mergers and acquisitions, where the driving motive is cost-cutting through reducing head count. Fifty-year-olds are normally the first to be offered voluntary redundancy.

Companies' justification for pushing out their older employees is that these people are in a better position to cope with unemployment. They are seen to have fewer family responsibilities and lower financial demands because mortgages and loans have been repaid. What this assumption fails to recognise is that this is a 'sandwiched' generation. A growing number have greater and more complex financial demands because of increasing life expectancy and the more varied nature of their personal life histories. This means that more fifty-year-olds are having to look after ageing parents. With women no longer prepared to look after elderly relatives in 'granny flats', paid-for residential care is the only viable option. At the same time, the increase in divorce rates means that many fifty-year-old men are having to support children from more than one live-in relationship.

The corporate 'push' also operates in a more informal sense. Ageism is rife in Britain and probably more so than in the U.S., Scandinavia or the rest of Europe. Some of this is built into corporate human-resource policies, but it is also evident in more subtle ways. As companies re-engineer their operational processes around teams and projects, the new cultures often reflect the interests of younger employees. Feeling marginalised in these young peer groups, older colleagues feel themselves under pressure to quit – a not uncommon experience in high-technology and media industries.

There are, however, also 'pull' factors that encourage some fifty-year-olds to quite their jobs. These people are largely managers and professionals who can afford to take voluntary early retirement. They are in stark contrast to those in insecure, low-paid manual jobs who have to work until they can draw their state pensions. Managers and professionals, benefiting from lump-sum redundancy payments and income drawn down from company pension schemes, are often time and cash rich. It remains to be seen whether company pension schemes will be able to afford such high rates of early retirement in the future.

But, while the good times last, early-retired managers and professionals are having the time of their lives. As the hippie generation of thirty years ago, many never really wanted to have full-time jobs. Needing income in cold climates, they took up careers in the expanding public and private-sector professions in the late 1960s and 1970s. Interestingly, they do not see themselves

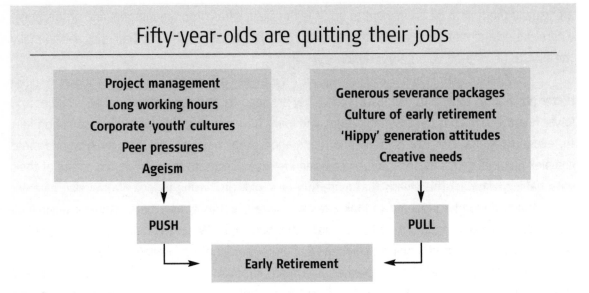

as 'early retired', but rather as moving into 'life after work'. That is, an opportunity to do the things that intensive employment and family pressures have prevented them from doing over the previous twenty or thirty years. These people have now established lifestyle role models that government policies will find difficult to shift. Despite demographic and economic trends that need people to work well into their sixties, a culture of early retirement has set in. Performance-related reward systems and project-management principles increase the intensity of work, creating stress and a work-life imbalance. Early retirement for affluent fifty-year-olds offers the ideal escape route.

The Scandinavian countries, when compared with Britain, have higher employment rates among people in their fifties and sixties. Is this because they have more effective family-friendly employment policies? Making employment more enjoyable and less stressful would reduce the attractions of early retirement for professionals, managers and others whose skills are in demand. Reducing mid-life executive burnout ought to be a corporate responsibility. It is only through this, backed up by effective, family-friendly legislation for all employees of whatever age, that the problem of talented fifty-year-olds choosing to exit the labour market will be resolved.

Achieving work-life balance through Internet technologies?

On the face of it, Internet technologies should solve the problems of work-life balance. The roll-out of broad band allows the home to be connected to the workplace. The adoption of laptops and personal digital assistants should enable employees to organise their work schedules in flexible ways and to execute many work-related tasks from the comfort of their homes. By working from home, working patterns can be made to fit in with domestic and household obligations. The ramifications stretch further than this. If there were widespread take-up of these technologies, the day-to-day commute to central business districts could be reduced resulting in less transport congestion and environmental pollution. It would seem that quality of life could be greatly improved. The legacy of the industrial revolution that created a sharp distinction between home and work could be eliminated.

Work styles and working practices will become more varied than those of the Industrial Age, but these will hardly solve the problems of the work-life balance.

Unfortunately, the hope that Internet technologies will solve these issues is misplaced. Although the knowledge economy and the values of knowledge employees shape the predominant culture, there are many employees who cannot work from home. By virtue of the nature of their jobs, as cleaners, maintenance workers, checkout assistants, teachers, nurses, social workers, etc, employees have to travel to work. Even so, there are growing numbers of people who could do more of their work-related tasks from home. Those who work with their brains, who are paid to exercise their intellectual skills, do not need to commute to work on a daily basis. Travelling to work every day to gaze into a PC screen seems absurd. A key factor that perpetuates these traditional working practices is the culture of management. In the old factories, employees had no choice but to travel to work. This created the assumption that employees' needed to be supervised on a face-to-face basis. In other words, they could not be trusted to be left alone to do their jobs. Even the introduction of piece-rate and performance-related reward systems failed to destroy this assumption. Through the detailed supervision of workers' behaviour, the value of their output could be improved through innovation in technology and working practices.

Workers resented these tight mechanisms of management control and, through this, a low-trust culture became established. It is this culture, migrated from the factory to the office, from the industrial era to the Information Age, that accounts for the low take-up of flexible working practices that Internet technologies can offer. Put simply, corporate leaders and operational managers do not trust their staff to work effectively if they are not on-site. For some jobs, they are compelled to give their staff personal working autonomy, for example, sales, marketing, transport and distribution employees. But, even for these people, communication technologies are being exploited to tighten up managerial control. This has been the major contribution of mobile telephones. It allows managers continually to check on their staff who are away from their desks.

Until companies are able to create high trust relations with their employees, the potential of Internet technologies to revolutionise work practices will not be realised. If this were to happen, operating costs could be greatly reduced through the opportunity to downsize office space. Maintenance, cleaning, heating and facilities management overheads costs could be reduced. With flexible working practices, hot desking could be introduced and employees would no longer assume that they have exclusive claims on corporate space.

But it is not simply a lack of management trust that prevents these changes. Employees, themselves, are reluctant to work from home. They prefer to maintain a physical distance between home and work. To be encouraged to work from home would be merely to extend the intrusion of their employers into their personal lives. Why should a room in the house be set aside as a study? Why should the behaviour of other household members be affected by workplace demands?

What is often forgotten in debates about flexible working practices and the work-life balance is that home working can make matters worse. It destroys what little refuge there is from the prevailing dominance of work demands. It intrudes upon 'switch-off' time and the development of complementary leisure activities and personal identities. Home working may allow for employees to be in better control of their time, to integrate their household and work-related duties but, against these benefits, there are the emotional and psychological consequences of never being away from their jobs. For employees who love their work, this does not matter, but for others, it creates rather than reduces stress.

Furthermore, the resistance to home working extends beyond this. Human beings are social animals. We prefer to interact with others on a face-to-face basis. E-mails and mobile telephone conversations do not compensate for this. It is a myth of telecommunications companies that their technologies substitute for the need for face-to-face relations. They do not. They fill in the gaps between meetings and facilitate rather than substitute for them. Until the

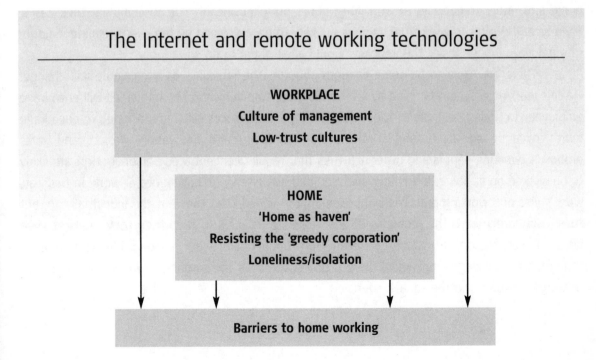

The Internet and remote working technologies

WORKPLACE
Culture of management
Low-trust cultures

HOME
'Home as haven'
Resisting the 'greedy corporation'
Loneliness/isolation

Barriers to home working

Manhattan disaster of 11 September 2001, business air travel continued to grow despite the capabilities of video conferencing. But video conferencing is always second best because the subtleties and nuances associated with face-to-face dialogue are lost. The arguments for home working also misunderstand the nature of creativity and innovation. Rarely are ideas developed in isolation into invention and innovative products. Creativity is a social process, the outcome of discussion, analysis, criticism and trial and error. Little of this can be pursued through virtual teams and remote working. It requires face-to-face contact and intensive sociability.

For these reasons, it is unlikely that the dreams of the technology prophets will be fulfilled. The capabilities of Internet technologies are unlikely to destroy the need for the workplace. Commuting is likely to continue and the home to be protected from the 'greedy' demands of employing corporations. In the modern world, the home is a refuge to be protected from the demands of line managers and project leaders. Employees are often forced to take work home and, more frequently, to work long hours both on and off-site to complete their tasks. Therefore, the offer to work from home is unlikely to be welcomed by the overwhelming majority of employees whose tasks, theoretically, would allow them to do so.

There are likely to be some changes though. The inflexible daily commute will change. Flexible working practices enabled by information and communication technologies will encourage employees to undertake more of their tasks at home. Workplaces will be redesigned to encourage more colleague sociability and, through this, creativity and innovation. Project and sales proposals, working papers and other activities that require concentrated personal effort are likely to be worked on at home, to be later analysed and discussed with colleagues at work. In this way, work styles and working practices will become more varied than those of the Industrial Age, but these will hardly solve the problems of the work-life balance. In fact, they could make it even worse as corporations try to intrude even more upon out-of-work personal lifestyles. It is as though, for knowledge employees, there is no escape from the corporate zoo. Not even in front of the television or on the squash court.

The challenges of life-long learning

It is becoming more necessary for us to take responsibility for managing our own lives. In the past, corporations offered us jobs for life. This followed a period of formal schooling that, for most people, ended in their mid- to late-teens. The structure of manufacturing had straightforward labour-market requirements. It needed these to do the productive manual work. And it needed others to supervise those who did the work. Selective education systems in Europe were geared towards meeting these labour market requirements.

The shortening of work careers demands that individuals are able to develop their creative talents in later life and after employment.

The stability of work practices has been eroded. Technological innovation demands constant skill updating. Processes of corporate change, brought about by mergers and acquisitions and the application of new technologies, have reinforced this pattern. No occupation is immune from these processes. It does not simply affect those working in highly paid, knowledge-based industries and occupations. Plumbers, television engineers, waiters, shelf-stackers and truck drivers face constant change in their job-skill requirements as a result of developments in technology. Even university professors are expected to be able to handle 'PowerPoint' presentation packages instead of reading lecture notes from behind lecterns. Students now expect sophisticated and illustrated handouts to go with these.

A changing work environment means that employees have to take responsibility for their own skill needs. They can no longer rely on the state or their employers to do this for them. It is for each employee to decide which skills they need in relation to their own career aspirations and job opportunities. It also requires the constant updating of interpersonal abilities. In the manufacturing company technical skills, as obtained through qualifications and training, were usually enough. In knowledge-based businesses, there is also the need to work with others, to cooperate in teams, to explain ideas, to negotiate and to communicate. Interpersonal skills have continually to be adapted to particular work contexts, leadership styles and team dynamics. These cannot be learned through traditional classroom methods. There can be no formal credentials that classify individuals in terms of whether they have these skills. Individuals have to develop their own self-learning strategies through developing personal portfolios of work experiences. They must develop for themselves learning agendas as they move from one employer to the next.

Self-learning does not just relate to work aspirations. There are also needs relating to more dynamic personal lifestyles. For those in their twenties through to mid- to late-forties, work and careers predominate, but after that new priorities begin to set in. For those in their early fifties quitting a job offers opportunities for developing new skills, pursuing new interests and developing talents that were irrelevant in former working careers. It means that knowledge workers never stop learning. With the extension of life expectancy into the mid- and late-eighties in Europe and the United States, life after work can embrace more than thirty years. A longer period, in fact, than the employment years. This puts a heavy premium upon self-education and the ability to develop personal interests that are neither employer nor market driven. Those who are unable to do this feel redundant and become psychologically depressed.

More varied personal lifestyles also demand more adaptive emotion and social skills. In the past, family relationships were more stable. Partners stayed together for longer periods of time. Divorce amongst those over the age of fifty was virtually unknown. Today, all relationships must be regarded as temporary. Nothing can be taken for granted. The gender revolution has made women more self-confident and self-reliant. Their greater economic rights allow them to quit couple relationships if their needs are not met. They will no longer put up with unacceptable behaviour from male partners. This has brought about a need for continuous personal development and self-learning among both men and women. They have to be more flexible and adaptive in their personal relationships.

These trends are becoming pronounced in the Information Age, which raises challenges for education systems and how these are structured and what they provide. Changes in work patterns and lifestyles require more flexible learning experiences. They demand that individuals are offered the opportunity to develop their emotional and social skills as well as those of a more intellectual or technical nature. Already there are developments in this direction in Scandinavia. In these countries, greater priority is given to interpersonal skills, working in teams and coping with flexible, ever-changing work practices. No longer is it regarded as possible to compress learning experiences into the first two decades of peoples' lives. The uncertainties of work and lifestyles demand constant updating of personal skills and capabilities. The shortening of work careers demands that individuals are able to develop their creative talents in later life and after employment. It forces people take on greater responsibilities for the acquisition of these skills. It also demands that governments incorporate within the bureaucratic delivery of basic literacy and numeracy skills, opportunities that allow people to identify and develop their own personal creative capabilities. The corporate zoo of the future will be even more varied than it is today.

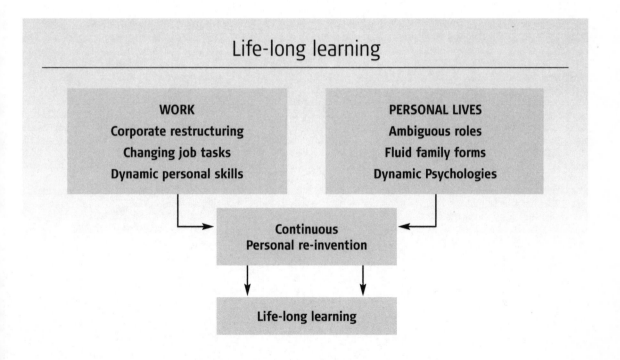

5

A zoo of lifestyle tribes

The end of age-old categories

It used to be the case that we could understand people's behaviour on the basis of some fairly simple categories. These were age, occupation, income and gender. Populations could be profiled according to these and products and services sold to them. Breaking down people into these groups as 'targeted' categories provided the foundations for advertising, marketing and selling campaigns. The whole media industry has been structured on the assumption that these are the key determinants of people's behaviour. It is on the basis of these targeted customers that films are made, magazines launched, television channels themed and radio stations focused. Unfortunately, the traditional categories of age, occupation, income and gender are no longer as effective as they used to be. They have ceased to be predictors of people's attitudes, values and personal lifestyles. People no longer spend their money according to their age or socio-economic status. Their leisure, eating, travel and lifestyle preferences are ceasing to be driven by these 'objective' characteristics.

It is a zoo of lifestyle tribes in which age, occupation, income and gender may be real, but of declining importance.

Knowledge workers are sophisticated people. They trade and work with their brains. They are expected to be intuitive and creative and to exercise judgement and discretion. They have to make decisions on the basis of reasoned analysis and logical appraisal. Irrespective of how far their talents and skills are used by their employing organisations, they are highly individualistic and non-conformist. This makes them cynical and suspicious of media messages. In their identities as consumers, they are inclined to reject and to disbelieve. Which means, as far as they are concerned, that advertising targeted at them is largely wasted. This psychological mindset makes them resistant to the appeals of advertising and marketing campaigns. Instead of accepting the media messages in taken-for-granted ways, they constantly assess and weigh up.

It is here that corporate branding is important. Knowledge employees read about companies in newspapers and business magazines. As individual shareholders, they receive annual corporate reports. As consumers, they evaluate the quality of products and services to determine whether they match the corporate promise. They assess the track records of companies on the basis of pollution and environmental scores, the treatment of employees and the traceability of the materials used to make the purchased products. With these consumers, corporate marketing and advertising campaigns are limited in what they can achieve. They can do little to change brand perceptions if newspaper editorials and television documentaries have disclosed unethical conduct, poor corporate governance or the exploitation of vulnerable labour. This is reinforced by the fact that, in an age of material affluence, consumers are in search of intangible qualities rather than tangible functionalities. The latter they take for granted. They assume that automobiles and household domestic appliances do not break down. They take for granted that products and services that they purchase will meet their material day-to-day needs. The intangible qualities that they seek are in relation to personal identity, experience and affiliation.

It is these shared experiences that provide the basis for the formation of lifestyle tribes. These have replaced the importance of demographic data for determining purchasing patterns. The sharing of experiences cuts across the old boundaries. Shared interests can be in relation to a diversity of activities ranging from sport and hobbies through to artistic pursuits. The point is that consumers create identities and interests that drive their purchasing patterns quite separately from considerations of age, gender and occupation. Lifestyle tribes are socially mixed and cut across old-fashioned marketing categories. The challenge for companies is to nurture these lifestyles around corporate brands. This is what loyalty cards try to do, as do television channels and national newspapers. More focused, targeted strategies, using experience-based rather than demographically determined data sets, are required if effective marketing and selling strategies are to be pursued. These need in-depth qualitative data which most companies are not prepared to resource.

The ramifications for the advertising, marketing and selling functions of media industries are significant. Old assumptions have to be abandoned and more sophisticated methodologies for reaching targeted consumers created. This requires advertising agencies to be more innovative

The end of traditional marketing categories

and imaginative, and demands that companies, in promoting their products, have proactively to construct their targeted groupings rather than relying upon traditional old-fashioned demographic criteria. It means that the creative industries must start to work for their fees rather than complacently repackaging and modifying taken-for-granted campaign templates.

This is not to say that occupation, age, income and gender are entirely irrelevant, but rather to state that these factors are no longer the predictors of attitudes and behaviour that they were in the past. This because of the changing nature of personal lifestyles. No longer can we predict future patterns on the basis of past practices. No longer do people behave as members of demographic categories and no more do brand, traditionalism and corporate loyalty play a key role. Consumers have become individualised, cynical, self-confident and even assertive in their purchasing behaviour. Old lifecycles and life-stage patterns that guaranteed predictability and stability in terms of how and on what consumers spend their money have been abolished. A number of factors account for this.

One is the increasing uncertainties and risks that people encounter in their personal and working lives. In the past, there was a high correlation between age, career progression and spending power. The older the person, the higher up the corporate hierarchy and the greater the

The end of traditional marketing categories

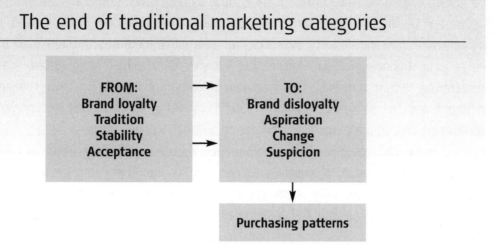

FROM:
Brand loyalty
Tradition
Stability
Acceptance

TO:
Brand disloyalty
Aspiration
Change
Suspicion

Purchasing patterns

disposable income. The giving of loans and mortgages for house purchase reflected this pattern, as did other forms of long-term credit. The expectation by both parties to the contract was that with time (and therefore age), earnings would increase. Today, predictable careers in an era of flattened, decentralised corporate structures are no longer available, destroying the certainties surrounding future earnings.

In addition, the destruction of corporate careers has also broken down assumptions about patterns of personal lifestyles and spending. Companies no longer expect their employees to behave as corporate ambassadors in their personal lives. Outside (long) working hours, whether or not these are executed on- or off-site, at the office or in the home, employees are 'free' to indulge in lifestyles and leisure patterns of their own making. The outcome is that corporate norms are less pervading. The employing corporation may be greedy in its demands upon the employees' time but not on their lifestyles. Corporate values that, in the past, encouraged conformity in personal leisure-based activities have been destroyed. Employees can choose to do what they want – during their 'free time' – so long as they deliver company results during 'acceptable' working hours.

There is now the search for individuality and the expression of 'difference' in personal lifestyles. 'To conform' is regarded as a statement of lack of character and personal charisma. To be admired, we have to be different, to behave as celebrities. Corporate leaders extol their skills as Harley Davidson bikers, jazz and rock musicians, mountain-climbers and so on. Some demonstrate their individuality by acting-out alternative identities through their participation in illegal drug taking, 'way-out' leisure dress styles or indulging in physically dangerous, life-threatening leisure activities. The message of corporate leaders to their colleagues is to be different and to 'express personality'. That is, so long as this does not prevent them from conforming on corporate premises and during 'normal' working hours.

These changes have been compounded by others affecting personal relationships. No longer do couples regard themselves as partners for life. There is a growing expectation that partner-relationships are only temporary to medium-term. Living together among twenty-year-olds can lead to split-ups and being single among those in their thirties. This can be followed by later serial periods of living in a relationship and then living alone. Divorce and personal break-ups occur in older age groups with growing frequency.

In the past, age-related lifestyles were pronounced. There were social expectations of acceptable dress codes, attitudes and leisure patterns associated with different age groupings. Today, the correlation between age and lifestyles has broken down. People in their thirties who live alone, have more in common with single people in their twenties than with other thirty-year-old friends with partners. A culture of 'youth' has been stretched from those in their twenties through to men and women in their forties. Equally, with increasing life expectancy, people in their fifties no longer feel old; they see themselves as forty year-olds with exciting futures.

Gender differences in lifestyles are also eroding. Greater opportunities for women in the workplace, the opportunity of having an earning capacity that enables them to take out home loans, allows them to choose to live alone. Higher education, professional training and corporate success create self-confident role models that other women now imitate. In both the United States and Europe, women's social identities are redefined. This inevitably redefines the identity of men. The outcome is a convergence, as well as confusion, in gender identities. No longer are men, men and women, women.

The end of age, occupation and income as the dominant drivers of spending patterns means that corporations have to create their own marketing categories. That is, their own lifestyle tribes around selected key corporate-brand messages. They need to construct their own marketing groupings organised around their brands in relation to products and services demanded by their targeted consumers. It makes corporate advertising, marketing and selling strategies more complex, intuitive and creative. It means that they have to convert consumer marketing data into corporate strategic intelligence. Software technologies, in themselves, do not allow this. Companies now have to respond to a greater diversity in consumer lifestyles.

Older women live with younger men. Women in their forties choose to live alone. Men and women who have lived with partners for twenty years or so, break up. Some men work until their seventies, others retire in their late forties. Postal workers, cleaners, corporate leaders and medical consultants find themselves at rock concerts, poetry festivals and sharing archaeological field trips together. It is a zoo of lifestyle tribes in which age, occupation, income and gender may be real, but of declining importance. Corporate data on consumers' past behaviour no longer provides the basis for anticipating their future needs.

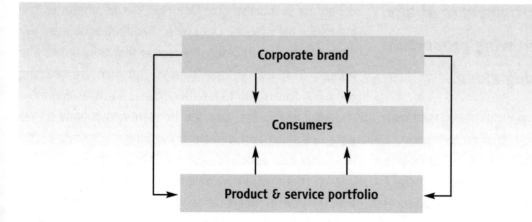

The demographic time bomb and the changing consumer

It is well known that people are living longer. It is less well known that there are declining birth rates in Europe and the United States, generating future shortages of young people, who will become employees and consumers of products and services. These demographic trends will affect the size of future markets. Equally as important, however, is the changing composition of households and the structuring of relationships and identities within these household units.

With the increase in early retirement and the dramatic decline of those working until sixty-five years of age, the outcome is a growing proportion of men living alone.

Firstly, there is the growth of single-person households, driven by a number of factors. One of these is the increasing life expectancy of men. Traditionally, women live longer than men. It is for this reason that they inherit the greater share of personal wealth. But men are catching them up. This is due to healthier diets, lifestyles and more frequent medical checks. Potentially life-threatening diseases can now be identified at early stages and treated. Medical technology is allowing both men and women to live longer. The fact that a large majority of those in their late eighties suffer from various disabilities that impede their quality of life is another matter. But the major reason that men are living longer, often outliving women, is through the greater incidence of early retirement. Retire at sixty-five and live until around seventy. Retire at or before sixty and live until at least eighty. With the increase in early retirement and the dramatic decline of those working until sixty-five years of age, the outcome is a growing proportion – up to thirty percent in some European countries – of men living alone.

A far more significant increase in single-person households is occurring among men and women in their thirties and forties. Traditionally, this age category constituted the 'hard core' values of family life. It was the prime target for advertisers and marketeers since their spending patterns were both secure and predictable. This has been destroyed by women and men choosing to live alone and by a far greater turnover of partners for both men and women. This age category now consists of a significant proportion of those who either choose to live alone, who are living alone between relationships, or who are compelled to live alone because their partners have left them. Single-person households now constitute the majority of households in the world's major cities such as New York, London, Amsterdam, Berlin, Stockholm and San Francisco.

These households tend to be clustered in specific geographical areas of towns, with their particular lifestyles dictating the nature of local housing, recreation and leisure amenities. They constitute lifestyle tribes that over-power traditional demographic variables such as age and income as drivers of spending patterns. Even the differentiation of single-person households as a consumer category fails to recognise the subtleties and diversities in attitudes and behaviour that can be found.

Among those in their thirties, there are clear differences between men and women who live alone. Among men, there is a tendency for them to be less fit and happy than those who live with women. They are likely to have isolated lifestyles, having only a few acquaintances rather than several close friends. They have little in the form of personal support networks. Their leisure patterns are reflected in a high incidence of eating out, alcohol consumption and spending on spectator sports. Single women, by contrast, have quite different lifestyles. They are healthier and happier than men who live alone and they are more likely to engage in a greater variety of leisure pursuits out of the home. They are more inclined to have extensive networks of close friends and to keep in touch with neighbours and family members.

Then there are single men and women who live alone but who are involved in long-term personal relationships. They protect their independence but, at the same time, avoid personal loneliness. This allows for careers and work-focused demands to take priority during the week without the work-life balancing conflicts that couples who live together often face. It is not until pregnancy that crucial decisions have to be taken about the nature of these domestic dual-household arrangements. Until then, it is possible for both partners to preserve their dual identities; both of independence and of emotional attachment. In addition, there are those single people who share accommodation. As a legacy of student days, flat-sharing becomes a solution for strangers arriving in cities and towns with uncertain job prospects. A 'wait-and-see' attitude encourages temporary living with others in order to underwrite high living costs on a relatively low job-starter income. In these households, there is often a domestic division of labour in which each person has responsibility for specific aspects of household purchasing. Personal lifestyles are shaped by the nature of these household's group dynamics. Diversity in the nature of single-person households affirms the ways in which age-old marketing categories are breaking up. More to the point, single-person households fail to constitute an homogenous marketing category. To capture these requires more than postcode data analysis.

This even applies to those households that, in the past, made up the core of advertisers' targeted markets. That is, husbands and wives with two or three children. The age of individualism has impacted upon the personal identities of both adult partners as well as their live-in dependent children. It has changed the dynamics of household purchasing patterns. In the past, women were the purchasers while men the deciders of how earnings should be spent. The reconstitution of gender roles and identities has destroyed this. Both men and women now choose and decide. They do so together and separately. But, equally as important, they do so to express their personal individuality. If all personal relationships are to be treated with caution and, at best, as medium-term, it is good personal insurance to preserve a sense of independent identity even in the context of live-in relationships. If in the past women saw themselves first and foremost as wives and mothers, today they regard themselves primarily as independent-minded individuals who, at particular periods in their lives, have child-rearing and partner obligations.

The family, defined as units of separate individuals, is being reinforced by the changing psychologies of children. Very early, they reject their dependent family identities. Ideas of personal independence become established pre-teenage. Children have seized the opportunities, offered by career and work-focused parents, to develop their own individualities. With their own bedrooms as their own territories, with televisions, stereo systems, computers and video games, they are now a major marketing category. With family members always on the move, but needing to stay in touch, it is no wonder the market for mobile phones has exploded over the past few years.

Consumer spending is driven by household characteristics. These have been transformed through the gender revolution, changing work patterns, increasing life expectancy and other lifestyle trends. They mean that corporate advertising, marketing and selling strategies have to be more sharply focused. Individuals pass through different and competing lifestyle tribes. Diversity and change describe personal spending rather than stability. To capture these in data and knowledge management systems is the corporate challenge. This puts customer relationship management at the strategic core of businesses.

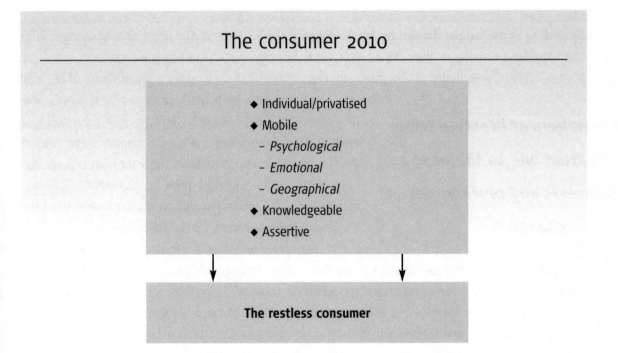

Who spends? Is it time rather than cash that matters?

Spending is no longer driven by basic demographics. One of the more striking changes is in the lifestyles of those in their fifties. This once homogenous socio-economic category has now become highly differentiated. Its fragmentation into different lifestyle tribes is symptomatic of broader social trends. A growing minority of this age group in Europe no longer has a full-time job. Through both push and pull factors, they have exited the labour market. Some remain working as freelance consultants, operating on a part-time basis. Others who have lost their jobs search for full-time employment. Still others have planned their finances to take early retirement and to enjoy life after work.

Transient members of lifestyle tribes, are moving from one to the next as their interests and preferences change.

Entrepreneurship is a growing feature of this age category. This is an attractive alternative for those who, through corporate restructuring, have lost their jobs. They tend to be former managers, professionals and others with various expert skills. With these, they identify trading niches in the marketplace. They continue to be work-focused with few changes in their personal spending patterns except that, free from the demands of their employing organisations, they can determine a satisfactory work-life balance. However, a growing number of the fifties age group consists of those who have planned their work lives so that they can quit their jobs in their early fifties. These are former employees who have accumulated enough financial rewards to retire. They regard quitting their jobs as an opportunity for developing new personal talents and skills.

These are often described as cash and time-rich consumers. They have both time and money to spend. With increasing life expectancy, they regard themselves as still young. Survey data for the United Kingdom shows there are few differences in the attitudes and values of those in their fifties compared with people in their forties. It is only on reaching the age of sixty that age-related differences begin to emerge. A number of factors account for this, including improved health and fitness and increased life expectancy. Those in their fifties do not consider that the best years of their lives have passed.

It is the men and women in this age group who spend more money than other consumers on travel, eating out and leisure activities. During the 1990s, their lifestyles have shifted from home-centredness to out-of-home sociability, leisure and entertainment. This has changed their identity as consumers. In the past, they searched for comfort and functionality in the clothes they wore, the cars they drove and the furniture they purchased. This has all changed. They are now committed to fashion and lifestyle products. Since they have plenty of time, they can pick and choose, and compare and contrast different products. They can play separate retailers off against each other. They are no longer the loyal customers of corporate brands. In the past, banks, car retailers and others could assume life-long loyalty. By attracting people in their debt-ridden twenties, they could be retained until they became affluent consumers in their fifties. This model of purchasing behaviour no longer applies to this age group. They behave as younger consumers, with greater product knowledge, assertiveness and bargaining self-confidence. But there is a difference. The spending patterns of those in their fifties are highly flexible, depending upon their membership of different lifestyle tribes. This fluidity of spending power is greater than among those younger household units whose purchasing patterns are restricted by mortgage repayments, child rearing and more limited budgets. Yet advertising agencies and the media still ignore them.

Also within this category, there are consumers who make up the 'sandwiched generation'. They have elderly parents who, aged in their late seventies through to late eighties, suffer from various disabilities. They require residential nursing and, often, twenty-four hour care. At the same time, there can be children, from a first relationship, at university and others, from a second or third partnership, still attending schools. For this sandwiched generation, spending patterns and lifestyles are squeezed between these cross-generational demands.

The break-up of personal relationships among those in their fifties is also increasing. This could be driven by early retirement and the recognition that the partners share few common interests. The outcome for this growing number of older men and women living alone is isolation

The consumer 2010

- Re-definition of 'age'
- Generation rolling stone
- The 'sandwiched' generation
- Time-rich/cash-rich
- From socio-economic categories to lifestyle tribes
- From stability to continuous change

and social exclusion. For men it can lead to illness and depression, as they have fewer support systems than women. This trend accounts for the growth of introduction agencies. Where do older men and women meet new partners? Certainly not in youth-focused discos, clubs and wine bars.

All these patterns are reflected in the social structures of communities and neighbourhoods. On one side of the street, there can be a fifty-year-old man or woman living alone. Next door, there can be a man in his fifties starting a family with a new partner at about the same time as he is becoming a grandfather. Further down the street, a fifty-year-old couple are looking after elderly parents as well as a grandchild who is the son of their unmarried, working daughter. Beside them, live an early-retired couple who, with money to spend and with few commitments, are able to travel, develop their creative interests and to engage in shopping as a central life interest. They are the members of the so-called 'mass affluent' that retail financial services target in their marketing campaigns. These variable characteristics mean that attempts to classify consumers according to their streets and neighbourhoods are becoming obsolete. The diversity of lifestyles driven by more complex personal and work experiences is generating more dynamic, ever-changing consumers. They refute traditional marketing categories because they are first and foremost independent-minded, assertive purchasers. They are the transient members of lifestyle tribes, moving from one to the next as their interests and preferences change. No wonder companies are falling over themselves to develop one-to-one marketing strategies and to implement customer relationship management (CRM) systems.

Personal branding: are we what we buy?

In a temporary world with transient affiliations, how do people shape their identities? In the past, membership of stable communities, neighbourhoods and family networks provided a sense of personal belonging and identity. It sustained more or less permanent feelings of security and stability. Networks of families, friends and work colleagues created feelings of attachment allowing people to cope with uncertainties and risks in their personal lives.

These structures determined the behaviour of individuals as consumers. They affected spending patterns and determined lifestyles. Personal values and aspirations were shaped by membership of permanent groupings of family, friends and acquaintances. Their networks were referent points for behaviour, patterns of consumption and

Companies now compete with each other to promote their own distinctive values in appealing to targeted lifestyle tribes. Indeed, the intention is to create lifestyle tribes.

on what and how money should be spent. They generated conformist patterns of behaviour as each person aspired to lifestyles specified as desirable by the relevant membership group. Within such networks, personal identity was also obtained by 'who you are' in terms of kin and background. It was a world of 'who you are', rather than of 'what you owned'.

Economic and social change have destroyed the basis for this traditional construction of personal identity. The end of life-long employment within particular communities is replaced by greater personal mobility. Ongoing corporate restructuring programmes, mergers and acquisitions have destroyed the capacity of individuals to establish long-term personal networks in neighbourhoods. Lifestyles are now characterised by frequent moves between communities and across geographical regions. People's sense of stability has been destroyed by corporate patterns, only to reinforced by greater uncertainties in their personal lives. The changing of partners, the psychological and emotional 'independence' of pre-teen children and the decline of traditional family forms have all added to personal feelings of insecurity.

The result is that the individual's sense of self is continually threatened. The constant changes they face in their work and personal lives create a permanent crisis of identity. 'Who am I?'; 'Behind all these different and ever-changing roles that I fill, is there a real me?'; 'I no longer know who I really am as I try to keep all these separate balls in the air'. These are the feelings of growing numbers of knowledge workers, of management and professional employees as they constantly strive to achieve their reward-related targets in an ever-changing work environment and shifting personal relations.

For some, the solution is to search for the inner self through psychotherapy and psychoanalysis, philosophy and religion. The growth of new religions among computer technologists, biologists and engineers can be explained in these terms. For others, the solution is through the search for the 'authentic' personal relationship. The seeking of a soulmate; a partner who will offer the opportunity for the expression of deep emotional feelings. In this, sexuality is separated from feelings of love. Sex is enjoyed by unattached singles on a Saturday night, while the search for pure love is more complex. This is why there is a higher breakdown in partner relations. It is a result of feelings of disappointment when the relationship is seen as not working. A turnover of partners is to be expected when emotional needs are not met.

For others, the solution to identity crises is through the acquisition of material goods and the expression of particular lifestyles. It is not so much a matter of conspicuous consumption as one of conspicuous personal presentation. It is the presentation of self through the ownership of material goods. It is through the ownership of these goods that I define who I am. In this, corporate branding plays a major role. In the affluent society, consumer products are highly substitutable in their functionality. Automobiles, household goods, fashion clothes, etc, are highly

The consumer 2010

The psychological state
- Self-focused
- Immediate
- Indulgent
- Temporary
- Cynical and suspicious

comparable in their tangible features. What differentiates these, and adds value to the consumer's identity, is their brand values. It is through these that individuals, in a temporary and mobile world, manage their self identities – identities over which they strive to have complete control. As such, these identities are not dependent upon changes in jobs or relationships.

From this springs the obsession with celebrity. Through the purchase of branded products, individuals aspire to celebrity in the context of their own personal networks. It allows them to present themselves as different, as somehow exclusive. Corporate branding becomes more

The temporary world of 2010

The search for:

- Identity
- Affiliation
- Risk-avoidance
- Health and well-being
- Quality of life
- Authenticity

complex in this consumer market. It is no longer merely a matter of promoting brand awareness so that everyone has knowledge of the products being promoted. It becomes equally, if not more, important to promote brand statute, reputation and the values surrounding the experience of using particular products and services.

This is leading to a general shift from product to corporate branding. By promoting general corporate brand values, companies hope to capture particular consumer lifestyle tribes and market a range of products and services to them. It is this which explains why many large businesses are rebranding themselves and adopting what appear to be obscure brand names. The intention is that these brands should not be identified with particular products or services. Instead, the objective is to have generic brands whose values allow a variety of products and services to be marketed. Companies now compete with each other to promote their own distinctive values in appealing to targeted lifestyle tribes. Indeed, the intention is to create lifestyle tribes. It is this that drives companies to give strategic importance to customer relationship management.

But do corporate branding strategies shape personal identities? It is doubtful. Consumers may purchase branded products for their identity-conferring characteristics, but brand values, as with jobs and personal relations in the modern world, are inevitably temporary. Individuals use branded products for varied and highly instrumental purposes. Beneath these, however, lies the authentic self. In the corporate zoo, the animals may present themselves in different ways to passing audiences, but do leopards ever change their spots? To assume otherwise is to attribute a misplaced over-importance to corporate branding strategies and the gullibility of consumers. They are far too astute and cynical for that.

From CRM to CMR?

Customer relationship management (CRM) is the contemporary corporate vogue. It has replaced the Internet as the topic for corporate events and for editorial discussions in business magazines. It is the logical outcome of a number of major trends from the past few years which compel companies to develop more focused and dynamic relations with their customers.

Consumers will dictate their terms and force companies to offer personalised prices for their products and services.

    A major factor has been the development of corporate information systems that allow companies to integrate what, in the past, were highly dispersed internal business activities. The increasing sophistication of software technologies has allowed them to re-engineer their vertically structured corporate silos to offer more horizontal, cross-functional services to consumers. The 'one-stop solution' is a term that is frequently used. Corporate, rather than product, branding is a reflection of how, through effective CRM, companies attempt to deliver ever-changing, bolt-on packages of products to consumers. More sophisticated software packages also allow companies to collect vast amounts of data on their consumers. This allows them to establish profiles of past purchasing patterns and to differentiate them into clusters, categories and 'lifestyle tribes'. The dynamic consumer requires a dynamic corporate response. Such is the promise of CRM.

    The reality is often quite different. One reason is that, contrary to corporate speak, the business process re-engineering for reinventing companies as customer-focused systems has been far from successful. Although software technologies may allow for integrated business processes, the overwhelming majority of companies remain functionally based and hierarchically structured. An integrated, single corporate customer-service call centre does not offer a solution to highly fragmented back-office activities. The break up of companies into measurable trading units, profit centres and operational departments also mitigates against this. So, too, does the quality of software systems. These may allow for the processing of complex amounts of customer data but, in themselves, they do not have the capacity to improve the quality of customer relations. In fact, in the longer term, they can have the reverse outcomes.

Retailers pride themselves on their ability to track the purchasing patterns of their customers. On the basis of this data, they organise the display of products on their store shelves and collaborate with manufacturers and distributors in inventory management. So far, so good. But there are two key weaknesses. Such customer-data warehousing only reflects what customers have purchased in the past and not – bearing mind their more dynamic, changing lifestyles – what they are likely to buy in the future. In this sense, CRM brings companies too close to their customers. By developing a detailed focus on their present-day wishes, future needs and future business opportunities can be missed. The outcome of this short-termism is high performance today and corporate decline tomorrow. A further weakness is that in the retail sector data warehousing is based on those products that customers have purchased in-store. It does not, by definition, include data on what customers have not purchased. This is either because they considered the products on display as poor quality compared with elsewhere or simply because they were not available. For store managers, this missing data is more important than the information in the data warehouse if they are to improve performance. In this sense, ignorance is bliss.

For there to be effective CRM, companies need to shift away from their technological dependency. In itself, technology never provides solutions. It is only a tool that can be exploited by human intelligence to offer strategic business opportunities. High-performing companies in the retail sector are those that use their customer data in conjunction with other more traditional management techniques. These include store managers spending a large proportion of their time on the store floor, talking with customers and staff. They observe purchasing patterns, watching how decisions are taken by customers, they consult their checkout staff and they constantly encourage verbal, face-to-face feedback.

Effective CRM requires human intelligence and imagination. Information technology cannot displace the indispensability of these human qualities. If it does, the result is highly bureaucratised corporate processes that reinforce the distance between companies and their customers. Consumers become little more than units of data on call-centre computer screens and the over-printed names on corporate mailshots. Instead of being valued and personalised, consumers reject the superficiality of these mass-marketing approaches.

It is questionable whether today's consumers want CRM. They generally regard it to be an intrusion upon their personal privacy, particularly when customer databases are sold on to other companies or used by the same corporate brand to market other products and services. The preference is not for CRM but CMR. In other words, **Customer Managed Relations.** Consumers do not wish to be managed by companies. It is they who wish to manage their relations with companies.

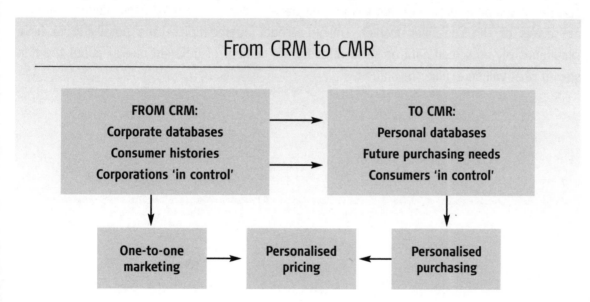

This, of course, was the case in the pre-information technology past. As we walk down shopping high streets and through shopping malls, we choose which shops to enter. We then decide whether or not to purchase and, as part of this process, to engage in negotiations. As customers, we are in charge. With CRM, consumers are passive agents in corporate marketing and selling strategies. With CMR, the roles are reversed and there is a return to the historic relationship between purchaser and seller.

The Internet has the potential for both CRM and CMR. So far the capabilities of the Internet as a trading tool have been exploited by the former. They have allowed companies to manage their relations with customers. The changing psychology of consumers, with their more sophisticated use of online technologies, is likely to reverse this trend. They will compare products and prices, search online and purchase off-line or vice versa. They will be able to construct their own databases of preferred suppliers and, in doing so, play one off against the other. The days of CRM are numbered and will be replaced by the practices of CMR. This will allow consumers to dictate their terms and force companies to offer personalised prices for their products and services. It will be a revolution that will first hit travel agencies and retail banks before it affects all sectors of the consumer market. Online account aggregation – the possibility to have simultaneously on-screen data on saver rates from a number of different banks –is but the first step in what will be a major revolution.

Online or offline?

Step back to 1998. Take a seat as a delegate at a business conference organised by a software company. Listen to the story. The Internet will change everything. It will bring about changes even bigger than those unleashed by the Industrial Revolution. It will completely change all aspects of our daily lives. We shall witness the end of the shopping high street. Commercial and retail property prices will plummet through declining demands. Shopping centres will be wastelands. Air, road and rail systems will be in decline through the reduced need to travel. And so the story continues. Why will all this happen? Because the development of Internet technologies will mean that we will no longer need to leave our homes. It will allow us to

> *Do website 'hits' represent anything more significant to consumers than flicking through magazine adverts in the dentist's waiting room?*

engage in purchases and transactions online from the comfort of our armchairs. Even the selection of our partners will be conducted over the Internet through online dating agencies, rendering as obsolete the need to meet future partners face-to-face! Remember the first Internet proposal of marriage in 1999?

Such forecasts were always going to be doomed to the rubbish bin. This is not to say that the internet and online trading are not changing the nature of business transactions. But to attribute to the Internet the revolutionary outcomes ascribed to it only a few years ago was greatly exaggerated and misplaced. The business model on which the growth of e-commerce was based was flawed for a number of reasons. It incorporated false assumptions about the change capabilities of technology. Simply because technological innovation has the capacity to allow things to happen, it does not necessarily mean that these *will* happen. Take the case of the Concorde forty years ago. It allows passengers to fly across the Atlantic faster than the speed of sound. But what history has demonstrated is that the great majority of travellers prefer to fly cheaper rather than faster. That is the reason for the commercial success of 747s over Concorde.

The same applies to the Internet. It has great capabilities for changing consumer purchasing patterns, but whether or not this occurs is dependent upon a range of social and cultural variables. In some countries the take-up of online shopping is likely to be restricted to distinctive lifestyle tribes. These are likely to be 'time-poor but cash-rich' men and women in the software, high-technology and media industries. These are the knowledge workers who developed the Internet in the first place. On the basis of their own particular experiences, wants and preferences they assumed that we all had the same aspirations. The dot.com boom was technology, rather than consumer, driven. Little research was conducted into the take-up potential among consumers. There was hardly any exploration into the likelihood of these consumers changing their established shopping patterns. A university sociology student would have been able to inform dot.com entrepreneurs that for most people high-street shopping is a shared, social experience. People may complain about congestion, queues and other inconveniences, but essentially they enjoy the experience and the buzz of gatherings of people, the face-to-face transactions and the out-of-home, social engagement. Purchasing products over the Internet via a PC or interactive digital television set offers little personal excitement by comparison, particularly when face-to-face

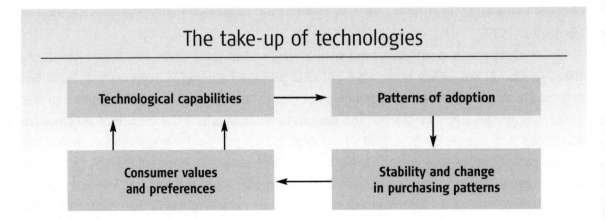

The take-up of technologies

Technological capabilities → Patterns of adoption

Consumer values and preferences ← Stability and change in purchasing patterns shopping is intermingled with meeting friends, entertainment and visiting new places. Shopping is an experience and not a functional activity. Something the dot.com entrepreneurs overlooked.

The rush of the major telecommunications companies into acquiring 3G licences by paying inflated prices at government auctions reflects the same psychology. Where is the business case that proves there is sufficient public demand to justify the prices paid for these? The now near-bankruptcy of many of these companies suggests that their business assumptions do not stand up to detailed scrutiny. 3G mobile telephony may allow for large amounts of video and text to be downloaded. But of what sort and for what purposes? For sports results, share and stock prices, but for what else? Certainly, there is a market niche, as demonstrated by the use of SMS services among young people. But is this sufficient to warrant the prices paid for 3G licences? Only time will tell.

The impact of national culture on the use of technology in purchasing patterns is also reflected in differences in the take-up of the Internet and handset technologies. The Scandinavian countries have the highest level of household Internet penetration in the world. With Italy, they are the greatest users of mobile phones. But the Scandinavians are more likely to communicate with each other through e-mail while the Italians use text messaging. Why is this? The Swedes and the Finns prefer to communicate with friends and colleagues when they are alone. Young people in Italy do so when they are with others. In Scandinavia, communications technology is used as a substitute for face-to-face contact. In southern Europe, by comparison, it is used to arrange face-to-face contact. So much for the naïve assumptions of those corporate presenters who, a few years ago, forecast the end of personal travel, high-street shopping and entertainment centres.

It is self-evident that Internet, digital, 3G and wireless technologies will have their impact upon shopping patterns. But this will be variable within and between countries. The challenge for companies is to identify what these are and then to develop compatible online and offline advertising, marketing and selling strategies. Some products and services lend themselves to online and wireless transactions better than others. The paradox is that it is exactly these same products that generate the greatest consumer anxieties over fraud and security. For example, most financial transactions lend themselves to online trading. But cultural differences in trust and belief in the robustness of corporate security and data management systems vary between countries. In Sweden, a major retail bank has ninety-four percent of its customers online. It is introducing online technologies that allow its customers to aggregate, on screen, their different financial accounts. This is hardly likely to take off in countries in southern Europe where consumers are more distrusting of banks and suspicious of fiscal authorities.

Online shopping is unlikely to intrude into those areas of purchase that relate to personal experience. Clothing has to be admired, touched and looked at and automobiles tested and checked. What appears to be emerging is the convergence of offline and online shopping practices. The prices of goods are compared online and then purchased offline. Alternatively, goods are inspected offline and then purchased at best price, online. But for the majority of consumers, the likelihood is that the Internet will function as a channel for information on products and services which are then purchased in-store. This makes the Internet, interactive digital television and 3G handsets corporate marketing vehicles rather than sales channels. Some lifestyle tribes may buck this trend but, for the majority of consumers, the end of shopping on the high street is not yet evident.

A range of social factors also account for this trend. Affluent populations are getting older and retiring from work earlier. Quitting jobs allows time for high-street shopping. This becomes the focus for personal decision-making, to replace that which is lost through early retirement. High-street shopping also fosters feelings of local attachment and affiliation. This creates a sense of location in what is an interconnected global village. This is in sharp contrast to the anonymity

Online or Offline?

Online	Offline
◆ Time-poor, cash-rich consumers	◆ Time-rich, cash-rich consumers
◆ Digitalised services	◆ Experience/sensory/fashionable products
◆ Standardised products	◆ Individualised preferences
◆ Researching the market	◆ Purchasing the products

of PCs and other forms of wired and wireless communication. It could not be more removed from the private, isolated world of the Internet surfer. The business models of the dot.com entrepreneurs were flawed because they were based upon misplaced assumptions of consumer behaviour. They started at the wrong end of the 'technology–customer' equation and exaggerated the likely outcomes. And they continue to stick to their misplaced assumptions. Do website 'hits' represent anything more significant to consumers than flicking through magazine adverts in the dentist's waiting room? If not, so much for the effectiveness of website marketing for generating online corporate sales.

Cynical citizens:
the changing citizen mix

Are private and public-sector organisations the same?

Public accountability forces government organisations to be bureaucratic. This is one area in which bureaucracies have many advantages over flexible, entrepreneurial organisations. There is a need for visibility and transparency of processes to ensure that all citizens are equally and

Efficiency and effectivity are not the same. Profit-making companies are driven by the former, while public-sector organisations are shaped by the latter.

fairly treated. Tax-collecting procedures, the payment of welfare benefits and the care of children in residential homes, for example, have to be seen to be executed according to rules and procedures. There is little scope for the exercise of personal discretion of the entrepreneur because decision-making and the exercise of decision-making has to be bound by transparent rules and procedures. Otherwise, the outcome can be corruption, the misappropriation of resources and, in the case of

vulnerable clients – such as children and hospital patients – abuse and malpractice.

What this means is that public-sector organisations operate according to a rather different paradigm to that of profit-making companies. It is a misplaced assumption that public and private-sector organisations can operate according to similar management principles. For profit-making businesses, enhancing shareholder value through delivering goods and services that meet customer *wishes* is the priority. In publicly funded organisations, by contrast, the primary goal is to meet clients' *needs*. These can often be in sharp contrast to their wishes. Patients may wish to leave hospital early but to allow them to do so would be contrary to their health needs.

The distinction between client *needs* and customer *wishes* is the basic principle that separates the structures and cultures of government agencies from profit-making companies. The result is that the former only functions effectively if there are strong cultures of professionalism. Professionals are required to determine the needs of clients, while managers in private companies deliver products to market in order to satisfy the wishes of customers and shareholders.

With the use of internet technologies, it becomes possible for cultures of professionalism to be more effectively developed and client needs to be more effectively met. In many organisations, there are tensions between managers and the professional and technical experts. This is because, while the former are client-focused, the latter are more preoccupied with operating processes, monitoring systems and assessing the efficiency of organisational delivery systems. The outcome is that the managers are seen to be in control – a factor which professionals, imbued with ideals of personal autonomy, bitterly resent.

Over recent years, governments in most countries in Europe have attempted to restructure their administrative processes to make the behaviour of professionals more visible and accountable. The aim is to get better value for money from public services in societies where there is growing resentment among citizens about tax levels. Further, the demographic time bomb is placing greater demands on government funding as a result of ageing populations. Through increasing life expectancy, there are more older people with disabilities, illnesses and with welfare and care needs.

The demand for better value for money has heightened the tensions between public-sector professionals and their management colleagues. Drawing from the experiences of profit-making corporations, key success factors, performance indicators, quality assurance exercises and internal, as well as external, organisational benchmarking through the adoption of league tables have all been introduced.

On the face of it, these changes would seem to be entirely laudable. Why should not taxpayers get the best possible return from the public services that they fund? No one can possibly object to this. However, the application of what is considered to be good management practice in private companies can be counter-productive in public-sector organisations. The drive to greater efficiency can lead to a decline in effectiveness with the outcome that clients' needs are less likely to be fully met. Long hospital waiting lists are but a case in point.

This is well illustrated in the application of performance indicators. If schools are measured according to examination results, teachers, unless they are prevented from doing so, will eliminate from the tests those who are seen as likely to fail. If local authorities are measured according to the speed of their response to citizens' enquiries, they will install customer call-centres. Rapid response is assured, but citizens may still have to wait, as in the past, to have their needs met by the relevant professionals. And so it is with hospitals, the police and social services. Performance indicators, by their very existence, generate greater efficiencies. But at the same time, they can lead to less client effectiveness.

More importantly, these imposed criteria can offend notions of professional autonomy. They can create resentment over the relevance of the criteria used in performance indicators. Unless these are determined through negotiation and agreement with professionals, their outcomes for service delivery can be counter-productive.

In other words, line-management principles are not effective in enhancing the performance of professionals in public-sector organisations. The attempt to apply these leads to professional employees renegotiating their psychological contracts with their employing organisations. From commitment, they shift to developing a more instrumental approach. They exploit every opportunity to 'get back at management' and to subvert the imposed performance measures. They perform tasks as expected of them but withhold ideas that could lead to improvements in service delivery that would benefit clients, whether these are pupils, students, patients, children in care, prisoners or whatever. In other words, they dilute their professionalism and, instead, respond simply as payroll employees. This, in turn, leads to a tightening of line-management control techniques and so the cycle continues.

The point is that efficiency and effectiveness of service delivery are not the same thing. Efficiencies can always be generated, creating a falsehood of high performance. These, however, can conceal declining effectiveness in client service delivery which, in turn, generates greater economic and social costs. School league tables, based on pupils' performance in examination tests, can lead to an overall average improvement in test scores. On the basis of these, it can be argued that a nation's general level of education is improving. But, if these same measures are the outcome of a relaxation of standards, the longer term outcome is the creation of a future underclass. Social and economic exclusion, as these occur in the United States and the United Kingdom, generate longer-term economic costs in terms of crime rates.

In the final analysis, public and private-sector organisations are not the same. They have different aims and objectives, and function with contrasting methodologies and paradigms, shaped by quite separate factors. These are concerned with the need for public accountability and the protection of professional autonomy in public-sector organisations. Efficiency and effectivity are not the same. Profit-making companies are driven by the former, while public-sector organisations are shaped by the latter. This determines their cultures and their operating principles. To confuse the two generates resentment and poor service delivery. The conflation of efficiency and effectivity is more widely accepted in political debate in the United Kingdom than in the rest of Europe. It is avoided to a far greater extent in France. Is this why the French public sector is so internationally admired?

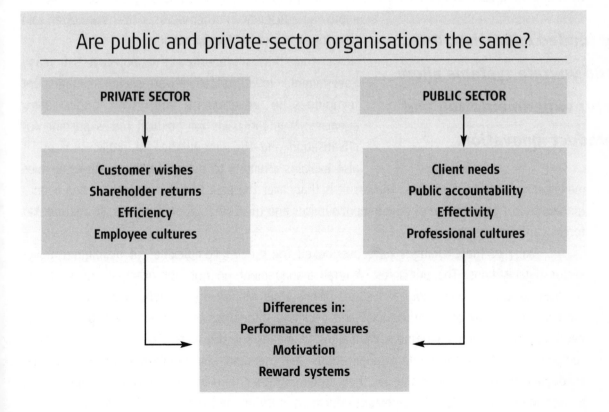

Are public and private-sector organisations the same?

PRIVATE SECTOR	PUBLIC SECTOR
Customer wishes Shareholder returns Efficiency Employee cultures	Client needs Public accountability Effectivity Professional cultures

Differences in:
Performance measures
Motivation
Reward systems

Are public-sector organisations really poor performers?

There is a widespread assumption in many countries that the public sector lags behind privately owned companies. Government agencies are viewed as lacking the management skills of their corporate counterparts. They are often seen as less productive and to offer more scope for improving efficiency. In other words, citizens are often told that they get poor value for money.

Publicly funded education, arts, health and welfare systems allow for greater experimentation and product innovation.

It is this that underwrites the objective of many governments to introduce private-sector management techniques in government and other public-sector agencies. It is the basis for political forces pushing for privatisation and the deregulation of public services. It also explains attempts to outsource to private companies many service-delivery functions. The result is that, over the past two decades, there has been a global wave of privatisation of government services and the deregulation of others, so that market forces can be more operative.

Many of these changes have overlooked the greater complexities of managing public-sector organisations. The principles of retail management do not, for example, apply to the complex human and technological systems of hospitals. Market-driven higher-education systems are characterised by cost inefficiencies and declining standards, as universities compete against each other in student recruitment campaigns. It means the duplication of selection processes, complex procedures for student applications and demands by employing universities that academics respond to the wishes of their students rather than to their needs. Nowhere is this more evident than in MBA management education in Britain and the United States.

These points overlook the fact that public-sector corporations are often more innovative than their privately owned counterparts. It is for this reason that much technological and scientific research relies upon private-public sector partnerships if long-term projects are to be pursued. In the pharmaceutical industry in Europe, for example, state-financed health systems provide the basis for clinical trials. As guaranteed purchasers of regulatory approved healthcare products, these same systems, either directly or indirectly, subsidise a significant portion of corporate R & D costs. Equally, in engineering, technology and telecommunications, research and development is highly dependent upon public-private sector partnerships. State funding underwrites development costs, which no privately owned company, accountable to shareholders, is able to do.

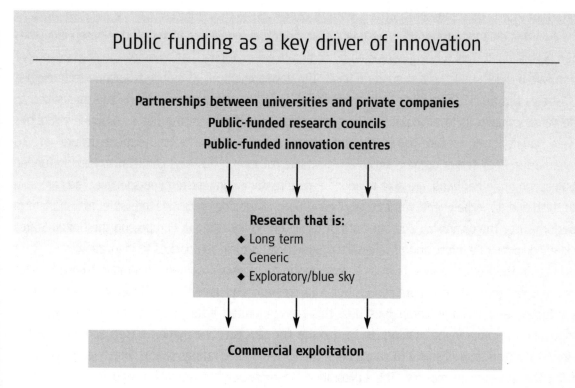

Public funding as a key driver of innovation

Partnerships between universities and private companies
Public-funded research councils
Public-funded innovation centres

Research that is:
- Long term
- Generic
- Exploratory/blue sky

Commercial exploitation

Such collaboration can take the form of sponsoring research within universities, but more generally it is through the operation of state-funded research councils. Through these, governments can shape the direction of scientific and technical research so that it is relevant to the needs of industry. That is, so that inventions will ultimately lead to the development of commercially viable, profitable products and services. Publicly funded research is also the basis for business start-ups. Universities are now focal points for the setting-up of business parks. These encourage public-private sector collaboration so that state-funded research scientists can convert their knowledge into profitable ventures. This trend is growing across the countries of Europe following the innovator, Silicon Valley. In determining the location of knowledge-based industries, universities of the twenty-first century are economic hubs and play a role similar to the coal and ore deposits of the nineteenth and twentieth centuries.

It is only through public investment that long-term innovation in knowledge-based industries can be sustained. This is being reinforced by corporate restructuring that assesses the performance of devolved business units on a short-term basis. The development of 3G mobile telephone technologies illustrates this point. The world's largest telecommunications manufacturers committed themselves to delivering complex, innovative products in a very short time-frame. On this basis, corporate valuations were inflated and service-provider expectations exaggerated. The subsequent failure of 3G manufacturers to deliver on time led to an inevitable collapse in business confidence. Publicly funded bodies, on the other hand, are able to adopt a more reasoned, longer term perspective. They are able to test and to experiment without city institutions exercising excessive pressure for short-term performance. The ownership and structure of television broadcasting in Europe and the United States clearly demonstrate public and private-sector differences in their approaches to innovation.

In the United States, television broadcasting is privately owned. This market-based sector has encouraged entrepreneurship through the creation and growth of a large number of small production and facilities companies. But this has generated little in the form of creativity and innovation in programme making. In fact, quite the reverse. The market-based approach in the United States is geared solely to consumers' wishes. Audience ratings shape what is commissioned from the programme makers. The outcome is an extremely conservative industry, reluctant to deviate from well-tried and tested programming content and format.

In Europe, on the other hand, broadcasting systems are either partly or solely publicly funded through licence fees. This allows for broadcasters to select broader criteria for programme commissioning than is available to their United States colleagues. Viewers' needs for information and education can be met, as well as their wishes for entertainment. In other words, broadcasters in Europe fulfil a key role in developing citizenship knowledge rather than simply concentrating on their wishes as programme consumers. Audience ratings are the criteria for programme commissioning. This allows for public broadcasting corporations to experiment, to innovate and accordingly, to offer a wider range of programming for a diversity of minority needs.

Publicly funded education, arts, health and welfare systems also allow for greater experimentation and product innovation. Markets have great strengths as distributive processes for meeting short-term consumer wishes. But people are also citizens. This demands that national economies also have well-funded public sectors. Perhaps this is why in Europe, there are national economies with highly developed notions of citizenship. In the United States, by contrast, markets and consumerism are dominant producing a far more conservative, risk-averse social structure. The high-tech gung-ho entrepreneurs of California are not representative of the stifling compliance of the broad mass of suburban America.

Wired government in an Internet age

The marketing strategies of software companies focus largely on the needs of business corporations. In doing so, they neglect the pressing demands of public-sector organisations and yet these lend themselves more readily to drastic restructuring through the application of software solutions and Internet technologies. In most countries of the world, government administrative systems are legacies of a bygone era. They reflect the requirements of citizens of an earlier industrial age. Not only this, but their design is the result of political processes rather than the changing needs of citizens. The outcome is the structuring of government processes and the provision of services that are outdated and becoming more redundant. This is not to say that public-sector organisations are not innovative. They are often leading-edge in terms of what they do in areas such as education, health and care. But it is their present-day structuring that leaves much to be desired. They may be very effective in service delivery but not particularly efficient. Internet technologies allow them to be both.

The Internet offers the potential for income-tax returns, benefit payments and even medical advice to be offered online.

In an information age, citizens need 'dot.gov'. Essentially, the task of governmental agencies is to gather, process and analyse information. On the basis of this, citizen intelligence is gathered that allows their needs to be met. This takes the form of planning and forecasting citizen requirements and setting up mechanisms for the delivery of services. For these reasons it could be expected that government administrative processes would be among the first to be converted to online and wireless technologies. If such strategies were in place, this would lead to the abolition of traditional government structures. Boundaries between central government ministers would disappear, as would age-old distinctions between national and local government. Today, this need for change is reflected in demands for 'joined-up' and 'open' government. The potential of information systems is that they offer opportunities for these demands to be met. Citizen databases allow for individuals to be tracked throughout their lives in terms of their education, health and welfare needs. The objection to this joined-up approach is that interconnected databases would produce 'Big Brother' governmental organisations. Not so if such data were accessible to citizens as of right and protected through mechanisms of public accountability.

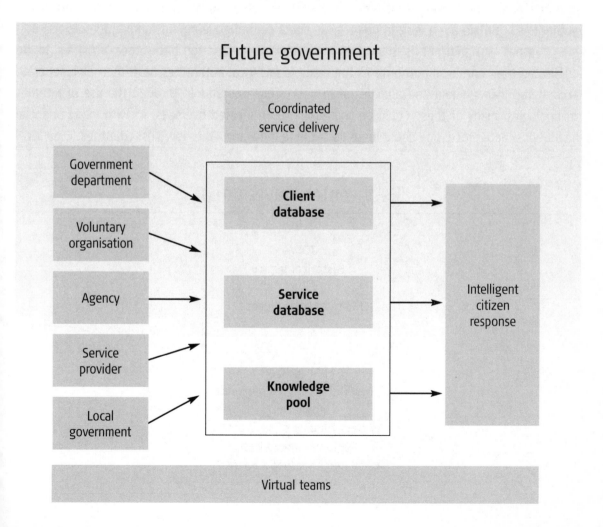

Future government

Coordinated service delivery

Government department

Voluntary organisation

Agency

Service provider

Local government

Client database

Service database

Knowledge pool

Intelligent citizen response

Virtual teams

No longer would there be a need for a distinction between national and local government bodies. Instead, there would be a convergence of service delivery mechanisms, some of which are monitored and supervised by nationally elected representatives and others by those elected at regional and local levels. Already, this is occurring in many countries. The need to meet the education, welfare or security needs of citizens is leading to the direct national funding of service providers at the local level, by-passing the traditional role of local authorities. Police and health authorities in Britain are a case in point, as is direct central government funding to schools.

What is significant is that it is no longer necessary for back-office activities to be duplicated from one local authority to the next. Today, local authorities have their own separate accounting, management and administrative back-office operations. Through the use of Internet technologies, many of these could be shared and even located overseas. As with many financial institutions, data processing could be undertaken in India and other low-cost countries. Even local

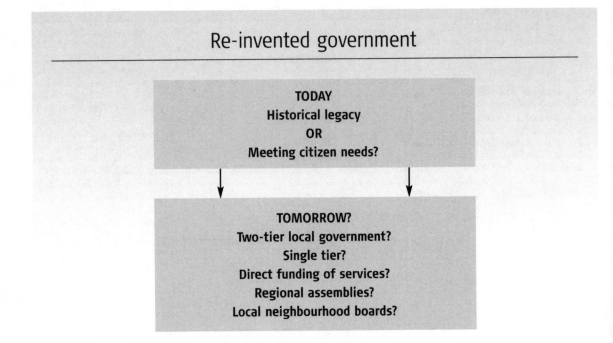

Re-invented government

TODAY
Historical legacy
OR
Meeting citizen needs?

TOMORROW?
Two-tier local government?
Single tier?
Direct funding of services?
Regional assemblies?
Local neighbourhood boards?

authority call centres could be shared. As far as citizens are concerned, they do not care from where back-office services are provided. They do not regard the primary task of local authorities to be job creation. What they want is low-cost, effective service delivery. Obviously, education, health and welfare services have to be provided on a local, face-to-face basis. What the Internet and software technologies can do, however, is to free-up resources to provide these more *effectively* and *efficiently*. They allow for closer professional-client interaction, with professionals having greater access to client data, often off-site, using lap-top and hand-held technologies.

Information technologies allow for there to be greater inter-governmental collaboration in the battle against international fraud, terrorism and illegal drug trading. The emergence of trade blocs, the growth of transnational corporations and global supply chains require a more effective response from national governments. This can only be achieved through greater collaboration, the setting up of international monitoring agencies and the sharing of data through Internet

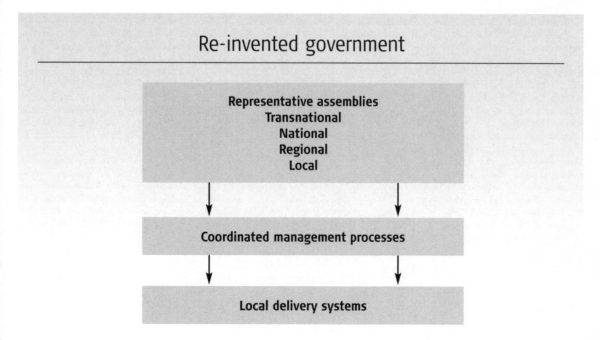

Re-invented government

Representative assemblies
Transnational
National
Regional
Local

Coordinated management processes

Local delivery systems

technologies. This leaves national governments with a number of major challenges. One of these is to develop new mechanisms of accountability so that all levels of government – global, regional, national and local – have institutions of representative democracy in place.

The shift towards virtual government seems slow in most countries. The most significant developments are in the Scandinavian countries. These are driven by the fact that household Internet penetration in Sweden and Finland is high. This offers the potential for income-tax returns, benefit payments and even medical advice to be offered online. As more and more services are migrated in this way, resources can be released for more effective face-to-face delivery systems. Online and offline services support each other in what is becoming a distinctive shift towards virtual government.

Schooling and universities online and offline

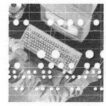

The development of Internet technologies allows for a complete rethink of how education is provided in the Information Age. Formal learning no longer needs to be focused almost entirely upon children and young people. Equally, the Internet abolishes the need for learning to be exclusively concentrated within particular locations. This does not, however, mean the end of schooling nor the end of universities. What it does mean is that the future roles of schools and universities, together with those of teachers and lecturers, will be very different in the future than they are today.

The greater use of Internet technologies in education systems releases teachers to spend more time developing the potential of each child

In the past, students attended universities since that was where knowledge was kept. The lecturer's role was, through face-to-face interaction, to stimulate student interest so that they could then develop their own understanding of academic disciplines through reading books. It is essentially a process of labour-intensive knowledge downloading. Internet technologies remove the need for this traditional approach. No longer is it necessary for information to be downloaded to students through fifty-minute lectures. It is not even necessary for students to attend lectures to obtain the hand-out notes. Now these can be downloaded through university intranets and the Internet to students' home-based PCs. On the face of it, it seems as though universities, as teaching institutions, have lost their historical purpose.

Far from it. Instead of lecture theatres, what are now required of universities are seminar rooms, laboratories and technical resource centres. With student access to information taken for granted, the role of the university lecturer is that of facilitator, encouraging students' personal

development needs. It means a return to the traditional role of universities. The historical role of both Oxford and Cambridge was to provide a monastic (college) environment for scholars, who could share their scientific findings and their philosophical ideas. It was an experience highly restricted to educated elites. What Internet technologies revolutionise is the opportunity for this experience to be enjoyed on a mass basis. Information can be downloaded offering greater opportunities for personal development needs - as future professionals, managers and technical experts – to be met more effectively on campus. Small group projects, working on scientific and technical experiments, encourage the development of skills needed for success in a knowledge economy. Universities return to their traditional role of developing personal creative talents and cease to be the learning factories they have become with the mass expansion of higher education since the 1960s.

If universities change in this direction, it is unlikely that three years full-time residence on campus will continue to be the model for most students. It may be the case for a minority of young people but for the rest of the student population, university education is likely to occur on a part-time basis. As people's employment and lifestyle experiences change, so too will their personal development needs. Attendance at local universities with enrolment on part-time, short-term courses will be the dominant mode. This is likely to lead to a convergence of online and offline learning methodologies with each reinforcing the effectiveness of the other; the acquisition of knowledge online being appropriated for personal development in the laboratory and the seminar room.

Universities have lost their monopoly of the higher education learning process. Television programmes can often provide in-depth information on the arts and social sciences in more stimulating, interesting and more exciting ways than traditional university teaching. In the past, universities rarely competed against each other in student recruitment. Today, the provision of higher education is a global business. In this environment, to offer solely the provision of a learning experience is no longer a competitive asset. This is taken for granted. Instead, universities compete on the basis of their social, recreation and technological facilities, as well as their global brand reputations. These are becoming more important in student choices as the brand of the university that they attend will affect their future employment chances. It is no longer a case of

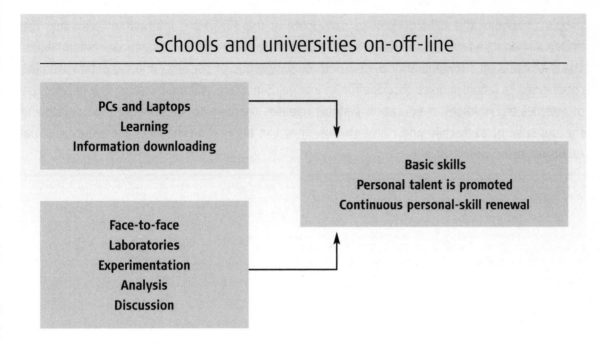

Schools and universities on-off-line

PCs and Laptops
Learning
Information downloading

Basic skills
Personal talent is promoted
Continuous personal-skill renewal

Face-to-face
Laboratories
Experimentation
Analysis
Discussion

simply attending university, but which one that becomes important. The brand of the university therefore becomes linked to employers' assumptions about students' employment potential.

The role of schooling can equally be transformed by the adoption of Internet technologies and the use of PCs and laptops. With the greater use of PCs in classrooms, information can be downloaded in ways more exciting and stimulating than by pupils simply listening to their teachers. The role of the teacher becomes one of working with groups of pupils in interpreting and analysing information. Personal learning agendas can be pursued according to each child's development needs. This can be aided by the use of laptops and remote technologies, allowing for linked-up and independent study at home. Homework becomes more interesting and enjoyable.

Schools and universities operate in broader social contexts. They both reflect and generate inequalities. In the Scandinavian countries, they are vehicles for maintaining social inclusion. These egalitarian countries have inclusive education systems that allow the broad mass of young people to acquire the skills needed to participate in the expanding information economy. The United Kingdom and the United States have education systems that reinforce broader inequalities. The outcome is an intergenerational, self-perpetuating group of socially excluded people who are condemned to labour-market participation in low-paid, insecure, vulnerable jobs. The greater use of Internet technologies in education systems releases teachers to spend more time developing the potential of each child and, through this, they can be vital mechanisms for reducing social exclusion in the wider society.

Economic clusters and local government

In an interconnected world, it is theoretically possible for companies to operate from almost anywhere. With modern communication technologies, supply chains can be managed from corporate centres, unhampered by constraints of geography. Equally, knowledge-based businesses no longer need to locate according to their proximity to physical resources. Their prime need is access to human capital and access to markets. This is in contrast to manufacturing companies in which transportation systems and the use of particular raw materials determine the location of factories. Knowledge-based businesses are more mobile. With Internet technologies, they can make use of human capital that is geographically distributed around the world. The use of software

Local authorities have to recognise that, in order to to attract and retain economic clusters, they have to compete on a global basis.

subcontractors in India, Australia, Costa Rica and Siberia are examples of this. Yet companies continue to cluster in particular locations. In this, they shape the demand for local facilities and, therefore, the role of local government. Why is this?

The clustering of economic activities within particular geographical regions is not, of course, a new phenomenon. It was a feature of the Industrial Age. The engineering businesses in the Midlands in the United Kingdom, the Ruhr Valley in Germany and the industrial districts of central Italy are cases in point. But knowledge-based industries also cluster despite the capabilities of information and communication technologies to disperse their activities. Global financial businesses are located in New York, London, Tokyo and Frankfurt; the film and entertainment industry around Los Angeles; software and high-technology businesses in Silicon Valley in California and in the Thames Valley in the United Kingdom.

These geographical concentrations reflect the importance of tacit knowledge and face-to-face relations in business transactions. Although online communication now plays a central role, it has not displaced the human factor. Sociability continues to be a key driver of creativity, innovation and, therefore, competitive advantage. Corporate strategies are rarely formulated on the basis of the rational analysis of market trends through mechanistic modelling that can be put together without debate and argument. Corporate policies have to be flexible to changing market uncertainties and this requires dialogue and discussion. Video conferencing and e-mails offer poor substitutes for face-to-face encounters.

This emphasises the need for companies to be located 'at the heart of things'. These business locations have their own dynamic and momentum for growth. This puts particular demands on local infrastructures. Those who work in particular industries have specific lifestyle needs. The media industries have very different cultures to the banking industry. Software engineers and technical experts have lifestyle preferences different to those in the entertainment sector. The outcome is that the separate geographical locations of these industries will be reflected in differences in their amenities and infrastructures. What separates knowledge-based businesses from manufacturing companies is that lifestyle preferences, rather than the availability of resources, shape location. Urban areas are preferred, especially metropolitan centres, where there are restaurants, theatres, cafes and a wide range of leisure and cultural activities. These allow for the development of personal networks and business contacts. It is for this reason that companies are prepared to pay the higher rental costs of urban locations.

The role of local government is to meet the needs of business clusters as these are shaped by global processes. This means the provision of appropriate education facilities for meeting the skill needs of particular economic clusters. It demands that planning policies allow for constant business regeneration through encouraging entrepreneurship. It requires that there

Locality as business 'clusters'

- ◆ Quality of life
- ◆ Infrastructure
- ◆ Tacit knowledge
- ◆ Buzz
- ◆ Brand

is heavy investment in transport infrastructures so that traffic flows can be effectively managed. It also compels local authorities to provide diverse cultural, social and entertainment facilities that meet the lifestyle needs of knowledge employees.

This generates further responsibilities for local authorities. Knowledge industries generate demands for personal-service employees, such as cleaners, security guards, maintenance staff, waiters, shop assistants, bus and train drivers. These are low-paid jobs but viable business clusters are dependent upon them. The task for local government is to meet the housing and accommodation requirements of this diverse group, consisting as it does of not only single young people in temporary jobs and migrants, through to those permanently located with household responsibilities.

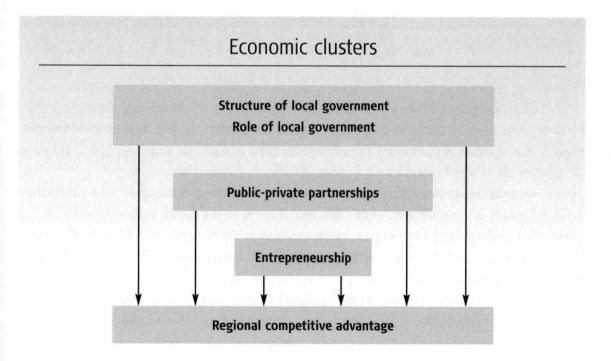

Economic clusters

Structure of local government
Role of local government

Public-private partnerships

Entrepreneurship

Regional competitive advantage

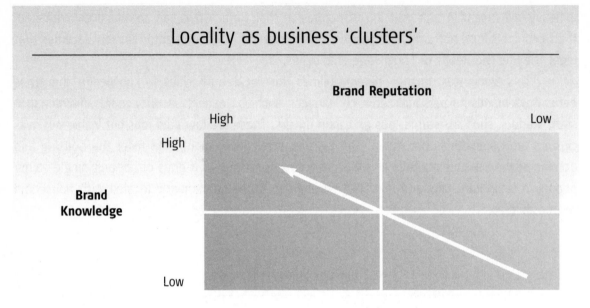

Locality as business 'clusters'

Brand Reputation

Local authorities have to recognise that, in order to to attract and retain economic clusters, they have to compete on a global basis. Companies can pick and choose between regions. It is up to local authorities to demonstrate their competitive advantage. Local branding becomes of prime significance.

Are local authorities appropriately structured to meet these challenges? How far do they meet the needs of corporations, employees and citizens in the global economic order of the twenty-first century? They are torn by conflicting demands. On the one hand, to be locally based, representative institutions. On the other, to provide the appropriate infrastructures needed by global-driven economic clusters. How do local authorities differentiate themselves and formulate strategies for amenities and quality of life to attract businesses in a competitive global context? It is here that private-public sector consortia and partnerships are able to play an indispensable role, but these can only be effective by operating within longer term regional planning strategies.

The demanding citizen and the rise of locality

Knowledge employees, as consumers, have high expectations. They demand value for money. They take for granted the delivery of quality products and services. This attitude spills over in their expectations of government. They regard the apparatus of government in just the same way as they treat supermarkets. They expect services to be delivered on time, as and when they need them. As citizens, they regard themselves as consumers, but in this case of services for which they are paying through national and local taxes. They expect transparency in terms of how tax revenues are collected and for what purposes these are used. They are more demanding about the efficiency and effectivity of service delivery in those areas that directly affect them, such as health, welfare, law and order, transport and education. Their interest in the provision of these services varies as they pass through the various life stages – living alone, looking after children, care of elderly parents and retirement.

In a world of growing mass communications and of globalised work experiences, the circulation of local newspapers continues to grow.

These citizens have little interest in how these services are delivered. It could be through outsourcing to private agencies, consortia of government agencies and administrative back-up provided in other countries. All that is important is a quality of service that meets personalised, immediate, but changing, needs. The outcome is the end of political ideology at both national and local levels. It means that local politics is seen as a growing irrelevancy. All that political parties can do is compete with each other in offering to deliver local services more effectively. But, despite political apathy, local attachment and affiliation is becoming more important. The work experience of knowledge employees may be shaped by forces of economic globalisation but they attach greater importance to where they live. As assertive citizens, they expect quality of life for themselves and other household members. In a global economy, it is largely the responsibility of local authorities to provide this.

In the past, citizens were tied to spending most of their lives in specific communities. They learned their skills through working for local employers. These were largely employer-, machine- and even task-specific. This inhibited their mobility between employers as well as geographically. Knowledge workers are more mobile. There is more movement between communities, from the countryside to provincial towns, from provincial towns to cosmopolitan centres. This is leading to regional imbalances in employment opportunities and in the provision of amenities.

Urban areas consist of more transient populations. Many people are doing jobs that are insecure and vulnerable. Corporate take-overs and economic downturn can rapidly transform personal employment prospects. In a more uncertain world, knowledge employees turn to themselves for security. They develop strategies for self-reliance. But they also look to their local communities. It is from these that they obtain a sense of personal attachment. If, in the past, these were mainly places of employment they now operate as psychological communities. 'Where I live' contributes to shaping 'who I am'.

It is in these terms that the role of local media has to be understood. It contributes to local branding. Local radio stations and, probably more importantly, local newspapers give localities their identities. News issues, advertisements and editorials generate a sense of community and brand reputation that shapes citizens' feelings of local affiliation. Some localities become known as good places to live because of their educational services. Others are known for their shopping and entertainment facilities. Still others are seen as ideal due to their quiet and relaxed character. Images are created that become self-sustaining. Each attracts particular kinds of people who are able to act out and enhance their lifestyles in conjunction with others with common interests.

Localities allow for individuals to develop lifestyles, friends and acquisitions that are quite separate from the world of work. They enable people to develop 'alternative' identities that are impervious to the threats of redundancy and other job-related insecurities. Participation in various locally based lifestyles allows for psychological buffers to be constructed against the greedy demands of employing organisations. The failure to achieve Q4 sales targets can be compensated for by being the star player in the local soccer club or the key performer in the amateur dramatics society. Community based activities allow for non-work creative skills to be nurtured and to be even more fully developed in the years after work, following early retirement (or corporate redundancy).

This is a paradox of the Information Age. As the world becomes more interconnected, business transactions more technology driven, and employees' attitudes more cosmopolitan, communities and localities take on a greater psychological and social significance. Through neighbourhoods, clubs, associations, churches and other forms of formal and informal participation, they allow for the expression of individuality. They offer contexts for human dialogue that are removed from the compulsive, corporate behaviour demanded of employees in their workplaces. They allow for an escape from globalisation and the search for a more informal, local based identity. This is best illustrated by the fact that, in a world of growing mass communications and of globalised work experiences, the circulation of local newspapers continues to grow. Communities, as contexts for personal networks, continue to flourish in a globally based corporate zoo.

Locality in a global economy

- ◆ Personal face-to-face affiliation
- ◆ 'Authentic' non-work identities
- ◆ Communities of interest
- ◆ Infrastructures of services
- ◆ Community 'brand'
- ◆ Quality of life

The competitive advantage of nations: does size matter?

In the age of industrial manufacturing, there was a need for a large domestic market. Through this there were economies of scale. When it was saturated companies exported their products and services. This attitude of management still prevails. The domestic market is the basis from which companies look to the rest of the world. It shapes their business cultures and operating practices. This can be seen in the ways that large corporations operate. How many are truly transnational or international businesses? Their headquarters, the composition of their main boards and their senior management teams remain domestically based. But, in the Information Age and with the rapid adoption of Internet technologies, forces of globalisation are beginning to destroy this concept. Many large companies are building transnational management teams. How are countries to compete if they are to provide attractive locations for the world's major companies? How are they to provide favourable conditions for entrepreneurship?

The animals in the corporate zoo perform better if they are well looked after in clean, well-lit and ventilated cages.

The traditional view is this must entail low labour costs, weak trade unionism and tax breaks. For some business activities, this is undoubtedly the case. That is why there has been such rapid economic growth in China and the 'tiger' economies of South-East Asia. These are significant factors that are taken into account when setting up factories that produce standardised, high-volume products and services. With short product lifecycles and with a heavy emphasis on the economies of large-scale technologies, comparative labour costs are at a premium.

However, in knowledge-based information businesses, this is not the case. Labour costs pale into insignificance when compared with the need to utilise brain power for competitive advantage. In the context of increasing globalisation, smaller national economies have a number of advantages over those of larger nation-states. For a start, they are more likely to have cultures of 'community' and 'cooperation'. These spill over to models of organisation and shape cultures of management. Employer-employee relations are likely to be more cooperative and to have high-trust relations, setting parameters within which disputes are resolved. These high-trust cultures also encourage corporate commitment. These features are reinforced by broader political environments and shaped by national governments that are able to engage in more open dialogue with citizens. They allow for greater grass-roots participation and for the links between political decisions and personal life chances to be more transparent. In other words, politicians are forced to be more accountable. In these circumstances individuals, as human capital assets, are likely to be more highly valued and respected, and their education and training to be seen as investments rather than as costs. Though improving individuals' productive capabilities, training will be regarded as the key means for generating economic growth and raising living standards. Each person is seen to have the potential for adding value to the welfare of all.

National competitiveness

	2000	1998
◆ Finland	1	2
◆ United States	2	1
◆ Germany	3	4
◆ Netherlands	4	3
◆ Switzerland	5	9
◆ Denmark	6	8
◆ Sweden	7	7
◆ United Kingdom	8	5
◆ Singapore	9	10
◆ Australia	10	15

Source: World Economic Forum, 2000

The Scandinavian countries offer good examples of these principles. Traditionally, they have very low levels of unemployment. Adult innumeracy and illiteracy rates are among the lowest in the world. They are highly egalitarian societies with, relatively speaking, low rates of crime and social disorder. There are no patterns of identifiable social exclusion of the kind found in the United States, the United Kingdom and the other larger advanced economies of the world. Sweden, Finland and Norway also have very high levels of taxation. Their employees are highly unionised and each country has a large public sector and a state-funded welfare system that absorbs a high percentage of GDP. Business is highly regulated through interventionist government that tightly constrains its activities. Both family-friendly and working-hours legislation is in place. Unions have an indispensable role in corporate decision-making. In short, the Scandinavian countries have all those features that many Anglo-American business commentators consider to be the antithesis of a positive business environment. A common thread that runs throughout their views is the need for low taxes, a curtailed welfare state, restricted government intervention and weak trade unionism.

And yet, the Scandinavian countries are at the leading edge of Information Age technologies. In the autumn of 2001, an OECD survey identified Sweden and Finland as having the world's most developed knowledge economies. They have the highest levels of household Internet penetration in the world and score equally highly in mobile telephone usage. They have world-beating records in registered product patents, R & D and product innovation. Their companies are leading edge in high-technology, new media and pharmaceutical and biotechnological research. Finland also has an impressive history of entrepreneurship and start-up ventures.

To be competitive in today's global economy, the information-based economies of Europe and the United States can only compete effectively through increasing the knowledge capabilities of their populations. This requires the development of education systems and life-long learning techniques. But brain power is not enough. There are plenty of intelligent people in every national population. For human intelligence to be harnessed for generating economic growth, it has to be motivated and managed. It requires those with intellectual intelligence to be able to collaborate with others in the pursuit of shared, corporate objectives. The educational systems of the Scandinavian countries encourage these capabilities. They do so by developing young people's emotional and social intelligence. If small countries are more competitive, it is because they are forced, in a global economy, to invest in people. From this follows government intervention, high taxes and well-funded public sectors. The animals in the corporate zoo perform better if they are well looked after in clean, well-lit and ventilated cages.

So what?

What is self-evident is that we are in a period of fundamental change. The institutions, social structures and life styles of the old industrial order are breaking down but there are uncertainties as to what are replacing them. New contradictions are emerging such as those of globalisation and the appeal of localism. There are forces of convergence shaping the social structures of different societies while at the same time, pressures that are reinforcing national, regional and local differences.

Many of these global processes have been driven by the growing dominance of the United States. But what is becoming more evident around the world is a growing resentment of the United States not only because of its political and economic might but also for the cultural values and ideals that it extols. This is in sharp reaction to the prevailing sentiments of as recently as two years ago. Then, at the height of the dot com boom, driven by the talked up hype of Californian entrepreneurs and their venture capital backers (to say nothing of the 'objective' analyses of 'independent' financial advisers), the world was going to be transformed by the internet. The United States was to be the leader in this revolution, bringing about a new dawn that would dismantle most of the old institutions. This has not happened and the world, especially Europe, feels let down. Today, the Internet is regarded as it should always have been; as a business tool.

But it goes further than this. Admiration for 'all things America' is now being queried because of the assumptions built into its business model. The focus on short-term rewards, a total pre-occupation with enhancing shareholder value with an almost total disregard for other corporate stakeholders (except in PR puff), is now recognised to be generating a too huge a downside. Fortunately (or, perhaps, unfortunately) it is only the United Kingdom that so fully embraces the value of this US business model. The other countries of Europe, especially in their different ways, France and the Scandinavian countries, are much more cautious. They recognise the shortcomings of business process redesign, the setting up of decentralised operating structures that are organised according to the principles of project management. The personal costs are seen to be too high with the excessive working hours, the erosion of personal lives by greedy institutions that are using the potential of remote working not to improve the quality of live of their employees but to extend their demands.

Even more so, the acceptance of this US-inspired business model is encouraging corporate irresponsibility. With the application of internet technologies and the single-minded focus on short-term profits, companies can shift their operations from place to place at the stroke of a pen. The American corporate culture has no moral responsibility to either national governments or local communities. It makes us all vulnerable to insecurities in terms of how and where we do our jobs, let alone whether we will even keep them after that next corporate strategic review. But the immorality extends beyond this. Structuring corporations as decentralised operating units with their own strategic plans, key success factors and performance targets, allows those at the corporate top to renege on their responsibilities to their employees. The buck always stops at the operational heads and the project leaders, allowing the corporate heads to hideaway, extolling their commitment to line management authority. But it goes further than this. With the compliance of their non-executive directors, corporate leaders can quite literally pillage corporate resources through apportioning themselves excessively high salaries, pension rights and share options. At worst, this business model allows for those at the top to engage in all manner of complex accounting transactions. They are accountable to no one and as the Enron case in the United States illustrates, the whole business can be brought to its knees without the knowledge of each of the separate operating units or subsidary companies There are probably many more Enrons to come.

No wonder the outcome among employees, who are not altogether daft, is to develop a totally instrumental, 'I'll get what I can out of this business' attitude. From top to bottom, long-term corporate loyalty goes out of the window. But at the same time it generates greater personal insecurities. A short-term pragmatic contractual relationship with employers makes the future uncertain with feelings of personal vulnerability and loss of control. Futures cannot be planned, decisions taken and life styles organised.

These forces are equally as evident among public sector employees as they are among those working for large corporations. The application of performance targets and key success factors geared to improving operational efficiencies can be counter-productive if they destroy ethics of professionalism. Devolved budgets can create operational 'gaps' through which vulnerable, 'uncooperative', 'difficult' clients as patients, pupils, children-in-care can fall. The pressures of performance targets encourages staff to queue for early retirement and sick leave generating skill shortages that have to be filled by overseas recruitment and induction training programmes. And so are private sector management models, as applied to the public sector, so efficient after all? Why should a young graduate become a social worker or schoolteacher if, with lower pay, they are expected to work under the same organisational regimes as in the private sector? The motive is to go for the money. Public sector organisations cannot have it both ways – to appeal to ethics of professionalism but then to impose business models that treat their staff as instrumental, uncommitted employees.

For Britain, the rejection of US-inspired models of management is particularly difficult because of its great cultural affinity with the United States. A common language and popular culture, adoration of the same celebrities and shared entertainment values, keeps the two countries together. After the 11 September, Tony Blair responded more as an American politician than as a political leader in Europe. The same forces that bind us to the United States keep us apart from the rest of Europe. This ranges from popular culture (with the exception of soccer), through to the ways in which we do business and design our private and public sector organisations.

Notwithstanding this, changes are underway. Forms of personal resentment are becoming more pronounced. People are not marching on the street, but they are taking early retirement, setting up their own businesses and refusing to be 'totally immersed in their jobs'. A culture of cynicism is becoming more pronounced, particularly among young people who will be the cadres of creative and knowledge employees in the future. Even those in love with their jobs, and who subvert the whole of their lives to them are only prepared to do so for limited periods of time. In short, U.S.-inspired management models are no longer seen to be the panacea for economic growth and efficiency. The personal and social costs are now being recognised to a far greater extent than only a couple of years. The bursting of the dot com dream has revealed other shortcomings of the American model.

It is perhaps symbolic of these changed times that the Leader of the Conservative Party visits Sweden to study its health service to find lessons for Britain. Whilst there, he would have noticed that it is the most advanced information society in the world, driven by government policies for social inclusion. Had he nipped over to neighbouring Finland, the home of Nokia, he would found a thriving entrepreneurial economy. This is despite high trade unionism, the effective implementation of working hours directives and family friendly employment policies. But of course, when he needs a hip replacement, he can always pop over to a French hospital. There he will find U.S.-inspired models of management rejected.

Britain is a society transforming itself from an industrial to a knowledge-based economy. But in the Information Age, work and employment will still be the pivotal axis around which institutions and life styles will be structured. Hence the ways in which organisations are designed have broader personal and social ramifications that this book has tried to illustrate. There are choices in terms of how these are structured and how governments and other institutions regulate them. For the past decade or so, Britain has chosen to admire and to imitate the United States way of doing things; that is, an unfettered market economy that sustains a high level of economic productivity but at a high price in terms of inequalities and social exclusion. Behind a façade of Hollywood generated excitement, it is a society of stifling suburban conformity with an obsession with self, appearance and banal celebrity. Is this the kind of society that Britain wants to be in the future? Or should we look to those other countries in Europe that are embracing the challenges of the Information Age but with perspective, social inclusion and quality of life as the endgame?

Index